ALWAYS
ROLLING
FORWARD

Copyright © 2018

Always Rolling Forward: The Power of Hope against Insurmountable Odds
Abdi Warsame

Published by: Rolling Forward Publishing

Editor: Blake Atwood, blakeatwood.com
Photographer: Michelle G. Marshall: mgmarshallheadshots.com
Cover Design and Interior Layout: MelindaMartin.me

ISBN: 978-0-578-42095-0 (print)

ALWAYS ROLLING FORWARD

The Power of Hope against Insurmountable Odds

Abdi Warsame

Contents

For my father,
whose presence in my life assured I had a life worth living

Introduction

Somalia is about the size of Texas—an ironic comparison considering I was born in Somalia and now live in Texas. My homeland sits on the eastern edge of Africa. Somalia shares a peninsula with Djibouti, Eritrea, and Ethiopia, which forms the Horn of Africa.

Over the past quarter century, Somalia has been described as a failed state, a pirate's heaven, and a hideout for Muslim extremists. As I write, Somalia is one of the six countries included in the US immigration travel ban—another irony given that someone I love would have fallen prey to this ban had it been enacted just one year earlier.

But we are not a people to be feared. (In fact, in February 2016, Somalia elected a Somali-American president from Buffalo, New York.)

For a moment, forget what you know from films like *Black Hawk Down* and *Captain Phillips*. Those portrayals fail to account for Somalia's proud history and tradition dating back thousands of years. In 2010, an archaeologist named Dr. Sada Mire of the University College of London discovered "prehistoric rock art created up to 5,000 years ago . . . at almost 100 sites in Somaliland on the Gulf of Aden in eastern Africa."[1] For instance, Somalis traded with the ancient world, including "Egyptians, Greeks and Romans [who] travelled to the 'Land of Punt' in the north-eastern Somalia

---

1   "UK archaeologist finds cave paintings at 100 new African sites," The Guardian, last modified September 17, 2010, https://www.theguardian.com/world/2010/sep/17/cave-paintings-found-in-somaliland.

to buy frankincense and myrrh."[2] We are still entrepreneurial by nature. Despite the chaos and destruction within the country since the collapse of the central government in 1991—a life-altering year for me—Somalis have developed one of the most advanced mobile telecommunications and banking networks in Africa. (Coincidentally, I have worked for AT&T since 2006.)

Somalis are not divided by what tends to divide a people. On the whole, we are not divided by race, religion, or language. Somalis are one ethnic group. But our fault lines are clearly demarcated in tribalism. Beyond the color of your skin, the practice of your holy days, or the accent of your speech, you are defined by your tribe. Clan-based politics colors every aspect of Somali society.

Tribal loyalty extends to public figures too. Somalis unsubtly allocate seats in the National Parliament according to tribe. The president and the prime minister must represent two of the major tribes. Key posts in the federal government are filled according to tribe. Wars are fought according to tribe.

Since its independence, Somalia has yet to break free from the clan-based politics that have resulted in so much bloodshed and loss. After decades of civil war since Siad Barre's regime was overthrown in 1991, Somalia is still reeling from the war's reverberations. Despite a desperate need to adopt ideologically based parties (e.g., Democrats and Republicans), Somali Parliament members are still chosen based on tribal affiliation above everything else. Parliament members do not represent their states or their districts but rather their tribes.

However, we don't have just two opposing parties. We have four: the Hawiye, Darood, Dir, and Digil & Mirifle. All of Somalia's presidents have come from the Darood and Hawiye tribes. Unsurprisingly, these two tribes were responsible for the Somali Civil War.

And the Somali Civil War is responsible for forever changing my life.

---

2   Mary Jane Harper, *Getting Somalia Wrong?: Faith, War and Hope in a Shattered State (African Arguments)* (London: Zed Books, 2012), 46.

Before I tell you my story, you need to know a little Somali history.

Mohamed Siad Barre assumed control of Somalia on October 21, 1969, ten years before I was born. As the leader of Somalia's army, he staged a bloodless military coup after President Abdirashid Ali Shermarke was assassinated by a policeman. With Somalia's Prime Minister Muhammad Haji Ibrahim Egal away on business in the United States, Barre saw his opportunity to overthrow a civilian government he thought was corrupt and inefficient.

Barre immediately banned all political parties and suspended the Somali constitution. He adopted Soviet socialist doctrine and rigorously applied it to the country. He confiscated privately owned corporations, jailed his opposition, and portrayed himself as the sole provider and protector of Somalia.

In other words, his title might have been president, but he was a dictator. My homeland endured his reign for twenty-one years, from 1969 to 1991.

A year before Barre's war would become my personal war for survival, I sat near the man and almost lost my life.

I was eleven years old and attending an event at Mogadishu Stadium on July 6, 1990, along with thousands of other citizens. Athletes from all eighteen states in Somalia were competing as part of an annual soccer tournament.

Amidst a round of boos, Siad Barre sat down in the President's box just a few meters to my right. In a few moments, he gave a speech that was immediately met with more jeers.

I could tell he wasn't used to such a reception. Everywhere he went, cheers and applause greeted him—more out of fear than respect.

As the volume on the opposite side of the stadium increased, so too did the president's frustration. It wasn't long before his bodyguards escorted him out.

Then I heard the last sounds I thought I'd ever hear at a sporting event.

Gunfire.

Screams.

Panic.

As bullets whizzed across the stadium, I ducked for cover. In the chaos, I couldn't tell what was happening. All I knew is that it wasn't good.

I later learned that one of Barre's "Red Beret" bodyguards had gotten spooked. Either fearful for his life or scared that he'd lose his life for not protecting Barre, the bodyguard began shooting indiscriminately into the oppositional crowd.

Later, I thought only a dozen or so had died—as if only a dozen could make such a political atrocity any better. Multiple reports revealed that at least *sixty-five* may have died.

Some had thrown themselves from the top of the stadium.

Some had been shot outside of the stadium.

More than one hundred had been injured.

I survived unharmed—that time—but likely only because I'd been sitting so close to Barre's box.

The Somali government denied the massacre. Our Minister of Information and Tourism called the shooting report "baseless . . . fabricated and concocted."[3] The Ministry of Labour, Sports and Social Affairs described the massacre as "a chance accident."[4]

It wasn't a chance accident. I know chance accidents. The Civil War would make sure of that.

The massacre at Mogadishu stadium was the final fuse to be lit. The flames of revolution, which had only licked at the fringes of the country, now set fire to the city's heart. Mogadishu was no longer content to allow Barre the kind of unfettered power he'd misused for so long.

Barre's regime felt the heat.

His soldiers began carrying out extrajudicial killings. Well-known

---

3   "POLICE OPEN FIRE IN SOMALI STADIUM," *New York Times*, July 11, 1990, https://www.nytimes.com/1990/07/11/world/police-open-fire-in-somali-stadium. html.

4   Ibid.

Mogadishu businessmen who were suspected of sympathizing with the rebel cause began disappearing on a regular basis. Civilian demonstrations were held against the government from July 14–16, 1989, and resulted in the deaths of four hundred people.

The powder keg exploded on December 30, 1990, in Gedka Jacelka, the "Love Tree" area of Mogadishu. Less than a month after armed conflict began in that neighborhood, Barre's regime would end—but not before forever altering my life.

1 King of Mogadishu

Saturday, January 12, 1991 | Love Tree, Somalia

"Abdi! Do you want to go to the city with us?"

My older cousins, Adun and Dhalin, stood in the doorway, smiling at their little cousin.

Adun looked at his brother. "I don't know, Dhalin. He's twelve. Is he old enough to go into Mogadishu with us?"

I couldn't tell if they were kidding or not, but I wasn't going to miss out on this opportunity. "Of course I'm old enough! I know those streets better than the both of you. This is *my* city in case you've forgotten. You're just guests."

My cousins, both in their early twenties, laughed and opened the front door. "After you, King of Mogadishu." They bowed.

I exited, then quickly stopped. "I don't know where we're going."

They laughed harder. "To get our stuff that's still in our apartments in the middle of the city. We know these streets pretty well too, little Abdi."

They knew I hated that name, but I so desperately wanted something to do that I let it pass.

While walking to the bus stop, I thought about how upset my parents had been earlier that morning.

Adun and Dhalin had just moved to our home a few days earlier. I was happy to have more family living closer, and I was thrilled that I'd have more cousins to hang out with. That meant more playtime. I'd gone over to a house my other aunt had moved into the day before to help them move in and wound up staying the night. But I made a near-fatal mistake: I forgot to tell my parents.

Well, it's not that I forgot. It's more that I just didn't tell them. I "forgot" to ask permission for lots of things as a child.

And did I mention this was in 1991, during the height of the Somali Civil War?

Somehow, my father figured out where I was. When he showed up at my aunt's house at 6 a.m., he was irate. "Where's Abdi?"

My aunt cautiously replied, "He's still asleep."

He barged into the room.

I awoke with a start.

Though normally a kind man, he was visibly upset. Loudly and tersely, he yelled, "Abdi! Why did you sleep here? Go home right now. Get the water buckets. Fill them. Bring them home. Nothing else."

I only replied with, "Yes, sir. I will get the water." Even though I was afraid, I was upset too. My father's reaction was beyond what my innocent intentions should have merited. *I'm with family! What's the big deal?*

I grabbed my shoes, sprinted back to our house, and finished my morning chores.

When I arrived home, I heard my mother trying to calm my father.

It wasn't working.

If I hadn't already known how much he loved me, it sounded like he was going to kill me. As an adult, I now know that his anger was more about the latent fear of being a parent who doesn't know where his child is—especially a child in a war-torn country being ripped apart by a civil war.

But I was still a child then.

Fearing the worst of repercussions—and after having dutifully finished my chores—my cousins and I had lunch together at our house. After lunch, they came outside. I was sure my cousins would be up to something, and something was always better than nothing, especially in Mogadishu.

My cousins and I waited for a bus we knew was never going to arrive. The war had disrupted so much of our lives already, and our public transportation system was effectively defunct. Nothing seemed to be working—least of all our government. But still we waited at the bus stop, just like everyone else was waiting out the war, hunkered down in their homes.

We hoped some brave souls would be headed from the suburbs into the city. Two hours later, just as we were about to give up on our escapade, a pickup appeared as if out of a dream.

Had I known what would happen, I wouldn't have been so thrilled to see that truck. Had I known that the danger of the city was far different than the danger of our suburb, I wouldn't have climbed into that truck bed. But I was twelve. I didn't think much of the conflict. I just assumed it would be over soon enough and our country would be back to normal.

The three of us jumped into the truck bed, carefree and happy to be heading into the city. On that bumpy ride, all I could think about was the heroic tale of adventure I'd tell my friends once we got back. Really, that was the reason I went with my cousins. Of course I wanted to hang out with them, but I truly wanted a fantastic story to tell my friends once we returned. Something like:

> When we arrived in the heart of Mogadishu, bullets
> whizzed by my ears, but I could hear them just quickly

enough to evade them. I barrel-rolled out of the back of the pickup. Heavy artillery exploded a house in the distance. I saw the shrapnel fly into the air. I think it even knocked out a guy. But I wasn't scared.

Then we saw one of Barre's men, all armed and angry-looking. I ducked behind a low wall, grabbed a rock, pulled the make-believe pin out of it with my teeth, and hurled it at the soldier. It landed right next to him, but it made him jump.

How's that for a rebel?

We ran into my cousins' building and grabbed their stuff as fast as we could. Just as we jumped back into the truck—which was already moving pretty quickly—a bullet cut through my flailing shirt.

Just look at the hole right there!

I thought I could cut a hole in my shirt to make it look like a bullet had gone through it. In seeing myself telling this story to my friends, I'd place my finger through that hole at the end, for emphasis—just to see if they'd believe me.

But my story would be of a different kind of heroism, one that was foisted upon me and was far too real.

———

As we drove deeper into the city, heavy artillery shelling exploded buildings far from the frontline of the war. I began to wonder, though not out loud, why we thought this was a good idea.

At least our driver knew what he was doing. He kept to the back roads because the main roads were either blocked or incredibly dangerous. He relayed to us that, just a few hours earlier, a house full of well-known, respected businessmen and city leaders had been shelled into oblivion. Muuse Boqor and Hussein Weheliye had been killed.

They had been working toward a peaceful resolution to the war that was engulfing Mogadishu and Somalia as a result of Barre's desperate last grab for power. They'd even attempted to convince Barre to step down, but he reportedly refused. The gathering of men in that house may have even been a last-ditch effort to save the country. With the deaths of those men, Somalia was likely headed for a disaster beyond comprehension. The fabric of Somali society was fraying along tribal lines, and it seemed no one would survive.

Not that I understood any of that as a child. All I knew is that we seemed to be driving *closer* to the bombing.

The truck rumbled on. My cousins and I jumped out just before we reached the Love Tree neighborhood.

As soon as we set foot on Love Tree soil, Adun placed his hands on my shoulders. "We must be quick and smart, Abdi. Don't slow us down."

I nodded. I didn't want to let Adun down. He was like a brother to me, and even back then I looked up to him. As a kind and down-to-earth guy who said a lot though he didn't talk much, I admired that he was a trader in a Mogadishu market, and I was impressed that we had to return to his apartment so he could get stuff that he personally owned.

As Adun took off running, Dhalin shouted behind his back, "We're going to my apartment first. It's near the front lines. Let's be careful."

As we ran, the stench of death crept into my nostrils. I wondered where it was emanating from until I saw indistinct clothing on the side of the street, flies buzzing like mad above the mound of rotting flesh. Dead soldiers lay scattered across the street, likely decayed by only a few days. I'm not sure if it ever crossed my mind that those men had died in this part of the city or that my fate could soon be the same. I may not have even thought that I could actually die until that moment.

Once near Dhalin's apartment, I heard the distinct sound of flying bullets again. This was no daring tale of adventure anymore. I didn't want to live this story, not even to tell my friends back home. When I first heard the bullets, all I wanted to do was leave. But Dhalin was still inside, gathering his belongings.

As Adun and I waited outside, the shelling began.

The structures around us crumbled under the onslaught. Built of wood and metal, those buildings could barely withstand heavy winds, let alone the brute force of heavy artillery. We had so little time to react before escaping that Dhalin wasn't even able to retrieve a pair of his shoes. We had to leave or risk serious injury—or death.

We didn't speak because we all knew instinctively what we had to do. Plus, speaking would have been moot: the shelling canceled any noise for miles around.

About three miles later, Adun ran into his house. Minutes later, he exited, but I couldn't tell if he'd taken anything. Considering what happened next, that's one of the thousands of nagging questions I still have about the day my life irrevocably changed: What did Adun take?

I eventually settled on the answer: cash. Why else risk lengthening your stay in a war zone for even a minute? Cash was hard to come by then, and it was the only item small enough that he could have stashed it in his pocket.

We then began the fifteen-mile walk home.

At 5 p.m., we stopped at my uncle Abdullahi's house. He was my mother's older brother and had helped our family settle into Mogadishu. He was alone, guarding his house at grave risk to his life, just like hundreds of other men throughout the city. He'd already escorted his family out, and his protective spirit couldn't help but plead for our safety too.

He begged us to stay with him that night.

He knew as well as we did that the chances of our survival while heading home were about to be cut in half. Sunset was less than an hour away. Without the light of day or the glow of ample streetlights, Mogadishu would be plunged into darkness within moments. When the night began, each warring side would stay its position because they wouldn't be able to tell who was who. They'd kill anything that moves. Even a cat knew better than to venture into the dark of a Mogadishu night.

But we knew that my uncle's house was close to the front lines. The risk of staying didn't seem to outweigh the risk of going, so, with my cousins leading the charge home, we said goodbye. With youthful naivete, we thought we could put enough distance between us and the bombardments before night fully fell. We assured my uncle that our fleet feet and faith in God would carry us safely home.

But God had a different plan.

As dusk quickly gave way to darkness, we approached a street engulfed in the distinctive sound of sniper fire. Reports reverberated off the half-crumbled buildings. Unlike automatic fire, sniper fire had a rhythm to it, almost like breathing. The pauses in between each shot made it seem like the soldier had killed his target, fallen asleep, or been killed himself.

What the pauses actually did was cause civilians like my cousins and me to think we could safely cross the street. I saw others hiding behind a building next to the street, crossing the intersection one by one. No shots were fired, and every person got safely to the other side.

My cousins and I ran across the street single-file. I was the last one to cross.

Again, thankfully, no shots were fired.

We cut through buildings to escape more live fire in that neighborhood. I'd never felt death so close before, as if every report of every bullet was the overloud ticking of a clock marking my remaining time on earth.

As we ran through the buildings, I remembered the name of the complex: *If iyo Akhiro. Life and Death.* I shook my head to dislodge what surely had to be a sinister coincidence. I silently prayed and asked God to shield me from the bullets.

We exited the Life and Death complex and came upon an open field— right next to a cemetery—just as shelling recommenced.

We ran like scared children. We sprinted across that field, trying to escape the same fate that had likely met most of the men and women in that cemetery. Three across, with me in the middle, we fled in terror.

We overtook two men carrying plastic chairs ahead of us, and then—

———————

Why am I lying on the ground? What's the ringing? Where're Adun and Dhalin? What just happened?

Dazed, I opened my eyes a few times, letting them adjust to the darkness. Once the world became clear, I saw Adun lying facedown, his right hip split wide open, blood covering the ground like an oil slick.

I screamed, "Adun? Adun? Adun!"

I saw Dhalin running in the distance. With as much strength as I could muster, I yelled, "Dhalin! Help! Come back!"

Dhalin shouted, "Are you still alive?"

"Yes! Help!"

Dhalin sprinted back to us and fell by his brother's side.

"Abdi . . . Adun is dead."

His words didn't register. Nothing made sense. *Adun was just running next to me. He's not dead. He's just hurt.*

I tried to run away, but my legs wouldn't let me. I squeezed my hands around my upper thighs. They were strangely soft and sticky. I touched my back and my fingers came back covered in blood. Something was very wrong.

Fearful that another rocket or bomb or bullet was about to assail me, I tried to get up and sprint away. My fight or flight response had never been so urgent, yet nothing in my body was allowing me to fly away. I couldn't move my legs.

Dhalin rushed to me. His eyes were wide and I could tell he'd been injured on the back of his head. He was asking me to do something, but my hearing seemed to falter. His words cut in and out like we had bad cell reception. Finally, he motioned to me by standing up and raising his hands into the air. I finally understood what he was asking me to do.

"Can you stand up? We need to get out of here."

Desperate to escape another shelling, I tried to stand, but my mind seemed like it couldn't remember how to move my legs. "Dhalin, I can't. I can't stand up. What's wrong?"

"Don't worry, Abdi. You're going to be OK."

Even then, I knew he wasn't answering my question on purpose. He was trying to protect me.

As he grabbed my left hand and began pulling me away, I pushed myself up with my right hand. He dragged me about ten yards away from Adun and laid me against a tree trunk.

I knew the sun would set in about thirty minutes. If we couldn't get help by that time, our chances for survival were slim.

That's when I finally realized the deadly extent of my situation: I might not make it to the morning. I might never see my family again.

Even as my pain was increasing by the minute, I prayed, "God, don't let me die without letting me see my parents one more time." The fear of never seeing them again outweighed the fear of not fully knowing the extent of my injuries.

I knew Dhalin couldn't physically carry me to safety, but I took comfort knowing that he wouldn't leave me behind either. It would go against the family honor system ingrained into every Somalian.

As these thoughts and fears swirled within my mind, a young lady opened her door in a house just across the street from where I laid.

Dhalin urgently asked for water.

She slammed the door shut.

Any dreams I'd once had went up like the smoke rising from the ashes of my country.

2 The Most Generous Man I've Ever Known

My father, Nur Warsame, passed away in December 2017, during the writing of this book. Without his lifelong dedication to me, the life I now enjoy would never have been made possible. I owe him an unpayable debt, and I will be forever grateful for his influence, care, and love. As you'll read in the coming chapters, I thrive today because of him.

My dad was my grandfather Warsame's fifth son, tall and handsome just like his father. My grandfather was a highly respected and admired figure in the Adaado community, the central Somalian city where I was born. My great-grandfather, Ugaas Farah, had been the chief of the Suleiman tribe that inhabits the area around Adaado. He was known to have been a just leader and beloved figure who had earned the admiration of his people because he was measured and firm in his judgments. By all accounts, Ugaas was impartial and never rendered a verdict without hearing both sides of the story.

It was to this storied line of intelligent, driven, admirable men that I was born into on January 1, 1979. My existence came about as a result of my mother's strong and independent will.

In 1962, my father, Nur, visited my grandfather's second wife in Adaado. (In the Islamic tradition, men are allowed to marry up to four wives.) While there, Nur met a young woman who was extremely beautiful and easily noticed: my mother, Hawa. She was a first cousin to my father's half siblings through my grandfather's second wife.

My would-be parents immediately connected, and my father knew she was the one for him. After a few *days*, my father asked her to marry him.

She agreed—but not before telling him there was another man who'd asked her father for her hand in marriage. Unwilling to marry that man, my mother had fled to Adaado.

Because my father came from a well-known and respected family, he went to my mother's father with some gifts and asked for her hand.

Thankfully, her father accepted him and blessed them to marry.

Otherwise, I might not be here.

———————

I am my mom's seventh child, the only son, preceded by four sisters.

Two of my siblings died before my birth. In 1974, my parents lost their two-year-old son, Abdisalam, during one of the worst droughts in Somali history known as *Daba-dheer*. "The Long-Tailed Drought" mainly impacted northern and central Somalia. "Some 19,000 people starved to death, and a quarter-million nomads lost most of their livestock, leaving them destitute."[5]

During that drought, my family lost everything. They sought help at a camp near Adaado, where rations had been distributed to drought-affected communities. My brother whom I never met didn't starve, but he got sick from powdered milk my family had gotten from the camp. Shortly thereafter, he died.

After the drought, my father realized there was little opportunity to raise his family in Adaado. A few days after my birth, he moved the family to the capital city of Mogadishu, 364 miles south of Adaado.

Adjusting to a big city was difficult. While my father was looking for

———————

5   Laura Heaton, "The Watson Files," Foreign Policy, last modified May 31, 2017, https://foreignpolicy.com/2017/05/31/the-watson-files-somalia-climate-change-conflict-war/.

a job, my uncle on my mother's side, Abdullahi, supported us. He was a businessman with the resources to support our family, but, more importantly, he genuinely loved us as his own children.

My father got temporary jobs, like working at a milk-bottling factory. But he knew he needed a stable job to support his family. From the 1970s until the early 1980s, Saudi Arabia was the favorite destination for Somali laborers seeking construction jobs. Saudi Arabia was experiencing a construction boom, and there were plenty of job opportunities. In 1980, my father got a loan, purchased his plane ticket for the three-hour flight from Mogadishu, and landed in Jeddah, Saudi Arabia. He quickly found a construction job near Jeddah. When he found someone whom he could trust who was traveling back to Mogadishu, he would send us money and gifts.

Remember: back then, there were no commercial banks or money transfers available to us. Even if there had been, that was when Somalia was governed by a socialist regime allied with the Soviet Union. Most of the private firms, including the banks, had been taken over by the Siad Barre regime.

Every couple of years, my father would come back, often unannounced. We'd only find him at the door of the house with a large bag full of gifts for everyone. Even now, every time I remember those days, it still brings happy memories. I often felt—and still do—that he loved me particularly, more than my other siblings. When he was home, he took me out to eat, just the two of us. I remember my first Fanta soda in a glass bottle that he opened for me at a nearby store that sold sweets and soft drinks—coincidentally near the Love Tree neighborhood.

In 1983, my family moved to the outskirts of Mogadishu to an area called *Waharacade*, which translates into "White Goats," under the government mandate. We were among the first families to move there. My father had moved us without hesitation because he loved the open space, the quietness, and the fresh air of the new area. He'd never liked living in the middle of the city. He built us a modest home there, and my mother ran a small shop that sold mostly fresh meat, vegetables, and other grocery goods at a nearby market. In 1988, my father retired from his construction job in Saudi Arabia. After that, my family was essentially living off of the income generated from my mother's work.

Obviously, we were raised on modest means. We weren't rich or poor. But my father made sure I knew what it meant to be generous. Years before I was born, he'd raised livestock. At some point, he'd farmed a little in Gidhes, a small town near Adaado. He'd offer the watermelons from this farm for free to anyone who was hungry, an unheard-of action in that period, especially from a man who wasn't wealthy.

He would later drill a water well at Gidhes, which didn't have a well back then. When he established the well, he didn't charge people for his water either. He didn't believe giving would diminish his resources. He always believed that whatever he had was a gift from Allah and, if he continued giving, he would continue to receive God's blessings.

My dad always believed that tomorrow would bring better fortunes.

When I was hoping I'd live to see the morning on that fateful day in the Life and Death neighborhood, I thought of my dad. I thought of him because I wanted to see him again, but I also thought of him because of what he'd taught me with his life and his words.

Tomorrow will bring better fortunes.

I had to believe that.

If I didn't, I'd die.

3 Station the Donkey

As I lay there by that tree near the cemetery, certain that I was dying, I couldn't believe that woman had slammed the door on us. We couldn't even get a drink of water, and she had to have known what a terrible state we were in.

Dhalin sat silently next to me. All we could do was watch the sun slowly fade away. Then as luck would have it, a compact car appeared as if from nowhere. *Who would even be driving into a war zone?* Dhalin stood up and waved them down. Fortunately, they stopped.

One man jumped out of the car. "Abdi, what happened to you?"

I recognized him immediately, a neighbor of ours from back home. I yelled, "Get me out of here!"

He quickly complied. With help from his friend, my neighbor carried me to the back of their car. Dhalin, who'd suffered a small cut on the back of his head and a minor leg injury, got into the back with me. Then they rushed us to a makeshift emergency room that had once been a pharmacy. In doing so, they'd taken us away from the fighting and closer to our home.

Upon being ushered into this ER, my ears were assaulted by the screams of the wounded. I saw caretakers stitching up severely hurt men and women. And I could tell by their shrieks and cries that no one was being given a sedative—very likely because no sedatives were to be found. The fear of not feeling my legs was suddenly replaced with the fear of being able to feel such pain.

Someone placed me on a table, and someone else began using scissors on my back, searching for shrapnel that may have entered near or in my spinal cord. I hadn't been sedated and I could still feel everything above my waist. The pain was unspeakable and unbearable.

I screamed, "Please stop!"

The man complied, bandaged me, moved me outside of the room, and laid me along a wall.

"Could I have some water please?"

Thankfully, someone gave me water this time.

The next thing I remember is seeing my cousin Asha's husband, Mohamed Hassan. I called out to him.

"Are you Abdi Warsame?" he replied.

"Yes," I whispered.

"Wha—What happened to you?"

So much had happened, and I was in so much pain, that I couldn't answer.

He just nodded in reply, gathered me up, and took me to his house, which was thankfully close by.

Their family didn't have any medicine. The ER hadn't had medicine. And, though I didn't know it at the time, I'd suffered paralysis from the waist down.

That was the most painful night of my life.

My aunt Amina, my father's sister, sat next to my bed throughout the night, patiently listening to my intense groans and trying to soothe me back to my fitful sleep. By dawn, she'd gone to my father's house to let him know what had happened. He quickly hurried over and took me home.

Upon my arrival, I was surprised at how happy my father was. He could tell I was in pain, but he was still *happy*. I didn't understand why until he told me: "You haven't lost a limb, and I don't see any major injuries." My father and my family members seemed relieved that I hadn't been seriously injured. They were all certain I'd make a quick and full recovery in just a few weeks.

Strangely enough, I had the same feeling. I thought, *In two weeks, I'll feel fine. I'll be going out with my friends again, regaling them with my heroic actions in the midst of war, and just about on the front line no less.* Remember, I was only twelve when this happened. Despite the pain I'd endured over the previous forty-eight hours, I was still optimistic about my future.

The fact that I couldn't move my legs mystified my family and me. On the third day following my accident, my father and a few relatives took me to see a local doctor. After he reviewed my injuries, he privately told my family that "there's no cure for Abdi, and there's nothing we can do to improve his condition."

When I saw my father after that consultation, he was silent. So were my other family members. Even at twelve, I knew that wasn't a good sign.

On the way back home, I pressed him with questions. All he'd say in response was, essentially, "Everything is possible by the will of God. You'll be fine, Abdi."

I knew I wasn't fine, but I still believed my father because I *wanted* to be fine. I wanted this nightmare to end soon. But it just became worse, and it would be worse for years.

The severity of my injury became obvious when I couldn't urinate on my own. My bladder would grow to the point of eruption. My family couldn't understand why I couldn't urinate if there was urine in my bladder. This new problem necessitated another trip to see a doctor, this time at a nearby hospital called SOS.

They laid me on the floor of the waiting room as my father found a doctor and told him about my particular problem. By this point, I hadn't urinated for at least two days, and the pain of that predicament was written all over my face.

The doctor rushed to me and pressed on my bladder. Nothing came out. He ran back into the hospital, then brought back a catheter, which he quickly inserted. Urine gushed out, filling half of the bucket the catheter flowed into.

Then the doctor, his face going red, got into my father's face. "How can you expect your son to feel when he should urinate when he has a spinal cord injury?"

My father didn't know how to reply. We knew nothing about spinal cord injuries. It's possible all he said was, "Spinal cord injury?"

Then the doctor, realizing our ignorance, became our first medical teacher. He provided us with more catheters and instructed us on how to use them. Then he provided us with a quick education on what it meant to have and live with a spinal cord injury.

Now that I knew what had happened to me, maybe I could better overcome it.

Everything is possible by the will of God.

———————

The Somali Civil War continued to rage around us. Though our house had been relatively far enough from the front lines, the front lines kept moving. As Barre's regime continued to lose neighborhood after neighborhood, they became more desperate. Their shelling attacks became indiscriminate. It seemed they no longer cared if they killed armed revolutionaries or innocent children. They were in the last days of waging a war they knew they couldn't win, and they would go down fighting.

Our signal to finally leave our home was less than subtle. A barrage of rocks and shrapnel from an artillery bombing flew over our house. Our neighborhood had finally become too dangerous. We'd witnessed that some of our neighbors had already evacuated, and my father made the fateful decision that we would too.

Of course, evacuating your family during a civil war outside of Mogadishu with a child who's just been severely injured presents certain logistical problems. But my dad's unwavering belief—everything's possible with God—motivated him to get us to safety.

On the day we'd leave war-torn Mogadishu, my father walked to the nearby market where our family had a shop. In vain, he looked for a car to transport the six of us out of the city as quickly as could be. But no usable cars could be found. So he found the next best thing. Well, maybe it was the next, next, next, next best thing.

When my father returned to our house, I didn't hear an idling engine coming to a stop. Rather, I heard a donkey bray and my father yell, "Station the donkey here!" My father and his younger brother, Ahmed, came into my room and took me outside, where they promptly placed me on the cart secured to our newly rented donkey.

My mother and sisters grabbed what they could from inside: cookware, clothing, a container for water, and some other basic survival tools. My dad locked the door for reasons I couldn't comprehend. *Was he planning to come back?* I was sad to leave my home, but I knew it would be better for all of us. We needed to get away from this regime that didn't care about its people.

As I bumped along in the cart, my family walked behind the donkey. Five miles later, we arrived in El Erfid, a completely rural area inhabited by ranchers who raised cows and goats. My father spoke to one of the ranchers and inquired if we could stay there for a few weeks until the fighting in Mogadishu quieted down or the situation somehow would change for the better.

Much to our relief, the rancher immediately agreed.

Knowing that we needed some kind of temporary habitat for the night that was coming too quickly, my father spotted a big acacia tree. My mother and sisters swept the ground, then my father laid down a blanket. My family had created as comfortable of a bed as they could for me on the hard ground of rural Somalia. Despite my ongoing pain, I was grateful for their care, and possibly even more grateful that no shelling would likely befall us that night.

We camped there for several days and subsisted on the food we'd had stocked at our small store in Mogadishu. My two middle sisters, Ureeji and Dhuuh, who were twenty and eighteen years old, respectively, at the time, often slept at the shop. They'd open it early in the morning despite the scarcity of shoppers. Yet my sisters were resilient. They were determined to get our family through this horrible tragedy we'd somehow found ourselves in. With my parents having to dedicate most of their time to my care, my sisters bore the brunt of adult responsibility, ensuring that we had enough food and at least some income. As is the case with my parents, I'm not sure I can ever repay what I feel I owe to my sisters, especially during this tenuous time in our family's history.

Just as it seemed like some normalcy, some sense of rhythm, was returning to our days, Barre's army shelled El Erfid a few days after our arrival. We were frightened that his long-range missiles had found their way to our retreat. Nowhere seemed safe. And with every explosion I heard, regardless of how near or far it seemed, my mind and body instantly jumped back to January 12, the day I'd been wounded. As a child, I lived in constant fear that I was either going to get hurt again, that I'd die, or that any or all of my family would get hurt or die. After all, it had happened to so many in Somalia. Our similar fate seemed inevitable.

All things are possible.

About a week after El Erfid had suffered the attack, I saw the Mogadishu sky light up with fire. It sounded as if every gun in the city were going off at the same time, an epic gunfight to end all wars. I wondered if Barre's regime were exterminating every last man, woman, and child in the city. I feared for my uncle who had remained to keep his home secure.

I barely slept that night, sure that Barre's face would be the first—and last—thing I'd see the next morning. His army would march into El Erfid and wipe us all out, even the sleeping kid who couldn't walk. Eventually, I fell asleep from exhaustion.

When I realized I was awake the next morning, I refused to open my eyes, remembering my fears from the night before. *Would the war come for us today—again?* But I knew I had to open my eyes.

When I did, I saw my father, grinning.

"Abdi, Abdi! Do you know what we saw last night?"

I shook my head.

"Barre has fallen. Barre has fallen. That was *celebratory* gunfire. The war is over, Abdi. The war is over."

I was so happy I might have cried.

All things *are* possible.

4 Not the End

"Take him back home." As he looked at my dad, the well-known doctor pointed at me still sitting in the idling car near the hospital's front entrance. "There's no treatment for spinal cord injuries. His condition will never improve. Take him home. Don't waste our time."

The doctor said a few more words I couldn't hear from my vantage point, but I could tell that my father was getting livid. I imagined that he was just as upset as I was. We'd been through so much and had already come so far. We wouldn't be deterred here. Not this close to actual help.

It was just a few days after the ouster of Barre's government. Now that the shelling had stopped and some semblance of normalcy had descended on our hometown, my father and I had ventured back into Mogadishu. We were at one of its main hospitals, which had formerly been a military hospital. But, ever since the war had killed, maimed, or injured so many, the hospital staff had been treating militiamen and civilians alike.

Abruptly turning away from the doctor, my father pulled me out of the car and into the emergency room. I'm not certain, but I'd like to imagine that my father stared the doctor down while he carried me into the hospital.

For all to hear, my father announced, "Treat this boy just like any other patient. He needs your help. I'm *not* taking him back home." Thank God for my father, my champion.

The staff obliged his command and found a room for me.

That hospital, the first of many I'd stay in for an extended time, was my home for the next ten months.

———————

My injury just so happened to coincide with the worst imaginable era in Somali history. For my money, I'd argue it was the worst imaginable time for any country on earth. For years, we'd been enduring a catastrophic civil war where neighbors who'd lived alongside each other for decades, whose kids had likely grown up with each other, were fearful of one another. Familial relationships by way of marriage were suspect. And if you couldn't trust your family or your neighbors, who could you turn to?

The government?

Unfortunately, there was no functioning government to guarantee citizens' safety. Somalia's civil war had destroyed or disintegrated our institutions of public health, education, safety, and law and order. Chaos was the norm. The most intolerant and violent members of society were its most vocal leaders. This conflagration led to unimaginable destruction throughout our nation, and very much throughout Mogadishu. The war had nearly obliterated our town.

At the hospital—at any hospital in the city—basic medical supplies were scarce. It was hard to find antibiotics, anesthesia, or catheters. (Well, we had a few from our previous doctor visit, but we certainly didn't advertise it.) Plus, the nearest rehab facility was near Degfeer Hospital, now known as Erdogan, but it had been closed since most of its staff had fled the city during the bombings.

Consequently, it's not surprising that my first extended hospital stay resulted in my further deterioration. Because of the firm mattress I was always lying on, I developed painful skin sores on the upper backsides of both of my hips. Several months passed before those sores healed. I would go on to lose much of my upper femoral muscles in both legs due to the removal of infected tissue.

My mother and father stayed with me during those ten months, alternating their stays every two to three weeks. My mother would often stay with me the longest, cooking and cleaning for me, and, maybe best of all, telling me stories from far better days. Still, I could tell by the way she looked at me and by the way my father spoke to me that it was difficult for them to see their son deteriorating.

Of course I felt sorry for myself. And the pain was often unbearable. But I hated to see the pain and the sorrow on my parents' faces. My parents felt paralyzed as well. There was nothing they could have done to alleviate my pain and suffering. When my mom and dad woke me in the morning and asked me how I was doing, I always answered, with a smile, "I am OK." I wanted to show them that I'd be OK. I was genuinely happy to have such extraordinary love and support from my parents and my siblings. There were many days that I cried, but I cried mostly silently and internally, sometimes under my blanket in the dark of the night. I knew I didn't lack their support or effort; rather, getting me the help I needed was beyond my family's capability. I wasn't a whiny kid. I always took life in stride—but a spinal cord injury was beyond anything anyone could comprehend, let alone a kid.

I desperately wanted to walk.

When I'd hear the doctors constantly say I'd never walk again, I didn't believe them. Maybe I was still in shock from my initial injury. Maybe I was genetically predisposed toward optimism. Maybe I was just a teenager who didn't want to listen to adults tell him what he could or couldn't do. Or maybe I was just a hurt child who wanted his former life back.

As my parents and I slowly came to accept our new reality, we never lost hope for a miracle. I imagined that there had to be some kind of surgery, or some kind of medicine, that could heal my paralysis. Maybe it wouldn't be available or possible in Somalia and I'd have to travel to the West for my cure. The three of us believed in that hope.

One day, my father approached two rather young-looking doctors at the hospital. "Is there a possibility for surgery to heal my son?" he asked.

One of them replied, "Well, we saw a piece of shrapnel in his back in an earlier X-ray. We could try surgery to remove it."

My father, encouraged by even the suggestion that part of my injury could be fixed, became excited. However, after consulting with a friend, he chose not to pursue surgery for me at that time. He worried that the potential for infection was too high and that these two doctors weren't well-known and didn't seem to have a proven record, especially for something as rare as a spinal cord injury in Somalia. Turns out, my father was right in his judgment: those two doctors had just recently been students in the medical college of Somalia's University when the civil war broke out. They probably just wanted to work on me more for their educational benefit than my healing.

Even then, we didn't lose hope. I never accepted the doctors' dire pronouncements over my life. Neither did my parents. The three of us wholeheartedly believed my future would still be bright despite its recent darkness. Hopelessness and despair would not overcome us. We were fighters of a different sort, and we would fight this battle together for as long as it would take. More than anything else, I believed our shared sense of optimism and belief in God would carry us through any looming difficulties. After all, God had gotten us this far.

Then, as if in answer to my unspoken, unknown prayers, my father's sister Barni visited us. She wheeled in a present just for me. The wheelchair was a beauty, at least in my eyes, and it was the best gift I could have asked for. This chariot would allow me to do something I hadn't been able to do since that terrible night in the Life and Death neighborhood. It would let me *move* of my own accord.

My father helped me into the wheelchair and pushed me into the hallway. With a smile so big that it betrayed my injuries, I pushed myself forward.

I'd forgotten what such a simple freedom movement was—right until I crashed into the wall.

I righted myself, but only to crash into the other wall. I was wobbling back and forth, left to right, unintentionally banging my new wheelchair down the hospital hallway, grinning all the way. It didn't take me long to figure out how to steer the thing. I wheeled it down the hall and toward the front entrance. I wanted the freedom that only sunshine can bring.

Expecting to fly out of the room and into the sunlight, I abruptly grabbed the wheels to stop myself. I was just a few feet from flying down the entryway steps.

Sheepishly, I asked my dad to help me down. He was already helping me before I'd finished my question.

Once down those small but insurmountable steps, I wheeled away from the hospital—not too far, but far enough to make myself think for just a moment that the hospital wasn't my home. My father stayed behind me, likely knowing I had longed for this singular kind of freedom for quite some time.

I breathed the fresh Somali air, now less redolent of gunpowder and rotting flesh.

I felt the warmth of the sun bathe my face.

I realized all was not lost. I was still alive, I still had my family, and I was getting help.

This injury would not be the end of my story.

————————

Saeed was the only other paraplegic in the hospital. He'd come to Mogadishu in January of 1991 to war against Barre as a USC fighter. During a battle in the south that summer, he'd suffered a paralysis-causing injury. Just like me, he couldn't feel anything from his waist down. Saeed was about a decade older than me, somewhere in his mid-twenties.

Almost every afternoon, I'd wheel past just a few rooms down from mine and enter Saeed's room. I felt like we could both use the camaraderie, but another part of me felt like he needed it more. While my parents were taking close care of me and my other relatives would often visit, it didn't seem that Saeed had *any* immediate family members. If he did, I never saw them visit.

To pour salt on his serious wounds, I'd also heard that he'd had a wife who had visited him during the first few months following his injury, but she no longer came around. I never heard why, but all I could imagine was that she'd left him for good after hearing so many doctors tell her that his injury was incurable.

I couldn't imagine having to endure something like that in addition to what the two of us were already facing.

Still, Saeed had a good spirit, and he did have friends who'd visit him. He wasn't completely alone—an aspect of my new life I wasn't even aware could be possible. I shuddered to think what would become of me if my parents ever left me.

Saeed was funny too. One night, a guy started trash-talking him. Saeed warned him to stop, but this guy wouldn't relent. Given Saeed's condition, perhaps this guy had thought, *Saeed can't do anything to me.* So Saeed asked him to come close. The guy came near. Then Saeed took his bag of urine and splashed it in his face.

That guy never again insulted him.

To fast-forward a few years, the last time I saw Saeed was actually in Mombasa, Kenya, at, of all places, my aunt's house. Saeed, along with his cousin, had somehow made it out of Somalia and into Kenya, where my aunt had given them a room.

He was more mobile than the last time I'd seen him, as he used a walker to get about. At that time, I wore leg bracelets in the afternoon. The two of us would walk around my aunt's house and discuss medical treatments. Saeed told me he had some sensation in his legs and that he could move his legs, fingers, and toes. This progress led him to believe that, given adequate medical treatment, his chance at walking again would be at least fifty-fifty. I told him that I hoped he was correct.

Unfortunately, I'd later learn that Saeed's immigration hopes had been dashed. Unaccepted for migration to Australia, where all his hopes for a better future rested, he deteriorated. As far as I was told, he was abandoned and died in Mombasa a couple of years later in a poor state of being—no healing, no friends, no family.

I couldn't imagine such a tragic end.

I have no doubt that, without the support of my family during those first tumultuous years, my story would have ended just like Saeed's.

In fact, my story could have ended just as this chapter began.

Two to three weeks after I was first allowed to stay in that hospital, my father told me what had enraged him so much when he'd first spoken to Dr. Ali Hobyo. My dad shared the words the doctor had essentially whispered to him: "Don't waste your time and effort. He's a lost cause."

In 1995, my father told me of Dr. Hobyo's passing. I felt sorry for the doctor, but I couldn't help thinking that he had assuredly forecasted my end and had tried to convince my father not to waste his time and efforts on me.

But I was the one who was still breathing. Only God knows when it is our time to leave.

5 Constant Movement of the Immobile

I woke to the sure sounds of war.

Had Barre resumed power? Or were some revolutionaries attacking us?

All I could hear was the unmistakable noise of gunfire and explosions.

My mother looked at me and told me to stay put. If it had been any other time, I might have laughed at her unintentional joke. But it felt like our hospital room was about to be attacked, so I just nodded that I was OK. She dashed out of the room to check on the other patients we'd come to know. She wanted to ensure that everyone else was OK too. Every now and then, with the resounding noise of terror flying through the streets outside, my mother would duck her head back in to check on me.

I was terrified, but I was OK. The walls around me had not yet crumbled, but with every new explosion, which certainly sounded like they kept getting closer and closer, I feared the worst was yet to come. And I couldn't believe that, after all we'd endured, I still feared that something worse could happen. *Wasn't the war over?*

We'd later learn that an ammunitions depot about a mile away from our hospital had been set ablaze. Rumor had it that scrap metal hunters had caused the fire. Who knows if they ever received the reward they sought for doing such an ignorant thing. This was during the summer of 1991, when famous historical statues in Somalia, modeled after Sayed Muhammad Abdulle Hassan, Ahmed Gurey, and Hawa Tako, had been toppled, sold for scrap, and exported to Dubai. In a war-torn country, the scrap metal business is big business. So, I guess a few brave yet idiotic entrepreneurs had decided to attempt getting as much scrap metal as they could at one time.

When the fire finally reached the first ignitable substance, it couldn't have taken long for the entire place to explode. With so much ammunition of all kinds, the streets *had* been filled with gunfire, shrapnel, and all sorts of deadly projectiles. The ammunition depot had been firing on all cylinders from each of its four sides. It's fortunate we had stayed inside.

While I'm sure the "attack" only lasted a few minutes, it felt like hours. And I'm still surprised that the hospital suffered few ill effects—aside from its inhabitants having to deal with even more terror.

But that wouldn't be our only night of post-war fighting. A real fight came for us just a few months later.

The reason why so many toppled dictatorships lead to civil war is that a vacuum of power exists in the wake of the deposed dictator. Now that the former leader has been removed or eradicated, someone has to take his place—and there are often many "someones" who will fight to the death to rule their country.

In September of 1991, two militias waged war against each other for the power that had once belonged to Barre. These militias were loyal to Ali Mahdi, interim Somalia president, and General Mohamed Farah Aidiid, USC Chairman. Ali Mahdi was a Mogadishu businessman and one of the financiers of the United Somali Congress. General Aidiid was a USC rebel leader. The USC rebel group overthrew Barre's regime in January 1991. Ali Mahdi was named an interim president at a conference in Djibouti. It was widely believed that General Aidiid never recognized the legitimacy of Mahdi's presidency. There was a continuing power struggle within the USC. However, early on, the two men united to rebel against the rearmed Barre regime, whom they saw as an existential threat. General Aidiid became the USC chairman in the summer of 1991, and the power struggle between the two men erupted into a full-blown war in Mogadishu in September of 1991.

As their fight continued, our hospital became a battle ground. Caught in the middle of a war that was not our own, we were forced to flee.

When she realized that we had to evacuate immediately, my mother wheeled me out of the hospital as fast as she could. But our rapid progress slowed to a crawl—well, a low-gear roll—when we met the hospital exterior's unpaved "sidewalk," steps, and uneven ground. I was certain I heard bullets whizzing by us. My mother pushed through, literally. The sound of gunfire seemed to halt for just long enough to get across the street. Maybe the militias had seen a mother and her wheelchair-bound son seeking safety. Or maybe they were all just reloading. I don't know, but I do know that, thanks to my mother's tenacity, we finally got to a relative's apartment near the hospital. We stayed there for the night. Thankfully, a truce was declared by the next morning, and the militiamen had returned to their bases.

My mother wheeled me back to the hospital. Thankfully, the streets were much quieter then.

Of course, if you've read this far, you know that the end of a fight in Somalia never really seems to be the end. Our hospital came under artillery fire during yet another battle between those same two militias.

This time, it was my father who had to wheel me out. As we had just cleared the hospital's grounds, my wheelchair sank into mushy sand, and it wasn't just sunk by an inch or two. I was legitimately stuck.

My father wrestled with the chair for a moment, pushing and pulling as hard as he could.

I tried to budge myself too, but the screams of those escaping around me, seemingly every person running away from the spot where we were stuck, had my rapt attention. I felt as if every part of me had suddenly become paralyzed.

Thankfully, an escaping hospital employee whom we knew saw us. He ran to us and helped my father push me out of the sand.

About a mile later, we arrived at Erdogan Hospital, where I'd spend the next few weeks.

All I could think was, *We haven't gotten far enough away. This never-ending war will find us here too. And we can only stay lucky for so long. Eventually this war will take more from us, as it has so many.*

I slept more fitfully than usual that night.

For someone who was immobile, I moved far too often in those first few years following my injury. We stayed at Erdogan for several weeks, until, of course, the fighting intensified. Our hospital, again, would surely come under attack. We feared for our safety every day, but the tension of imminent warfare seemed to increase the longer we stayed at Erdogan. In October of 1991, my father had had enough. We weren't just moving down the street or to a nearby neighborhood.

We were going home.

And not our Mogadishu home, but our ancestral home: Adaado, 364 miles north of Mogadishu.

We left the hospital under the cover of darkness and joined a convoy of a few buses guarded by lightly armored troops. That night, we camped at Lafole University, about fourteen miles away from Mogadishu. The following morning, instead of heading for Bal'ad, which would have been the fastest route to Adaado, we were forced to detour to Afgoye out of fear that the other militias would take us hostage.

On our way to Afgoye, we stopped for lunch at Buurhakaba. We'd traveled 112 miles on bumpy, unpaved roads. By the time we arrived in Buulebarde that night, we'd ridden another 195 miles. We only had 58 miles to go, but everyone on the bus seemed exhausted. That night, everyone got off the bus to find food and a place to sleep.

Well, everyone but me.

It would have been extremely difficult for anyone to help me off of the bus. It had been challenging enough just to get me loaded onto this bus with no wheelchair accessibility and no hydraulic lifts. So I remained in the bus, lying on the very back seat, while my father found food for us. He brought it back, we dined, and then we both slept in the bus. Before dawn, we were moving again.

But our journey wasn't as short as I had hoped. Due to the threat of kidnapping by armed militias, we were again detoured, except this time it required us to navigate a mountainous passage east of Baledwaye, the apparent city of kidnappers-in-waiting. We didn't arrive in Adaado until that evening.

Although we were exhausted and hungry, the sight of Adaado filled us with joy and relief.

My father somehow extricated me from the bus, then immediately hurried us to his late father's house in the city.

We were home.

Our home.

Far away from the war.

———————

I lived in Adaado for the next five months.

Were it not for my injury and the fighting that was still happening in our country, I could have called this time my first return to normalcy. But I always knew that normal would never be normal for me again. There was so much I needed to know and so much more I needed to learn.

One thing I learned that surprised me while in Adaado was just how many relatives I had. My extended family is huge, with uncles, aunts, cousins, and even younger brothers of my late grandfather who were still living. I would come to learn that they live across the globe too: in Adaado, at the border of Somalia and Ethiopia, throughout Somalia, and, as far as I know, in the U.S. the U.K., Kenya, Switzerland, Sudan, Canada, Qatar, Saudi Arabia, New Zealand, and South Africa. Looking back now, so many of my family members, in so many different places, played integral roles in my eventual thriving. I was and will always remain thankful to them for all they've done for me.

With the help of one of my younger cousins, Abdi Abdullahi, we explored Adaado. Back then, the town wasn't that big; I could wheel myself from one side to the other within fifteen minutes. Adaado had one water well that supplied the town's water. I remember watching the herders at night bring their camels, cows, goats, and sheep to the well. Then I'd look for the animals the next morning, but they'd have vanished.

Adaado was also experiencing a commercial boon of sorts, an unintended consequence of the war. Because of the fighting, Mogadishu's port was effectively closed for business. Consequently, Adaado received goods from the port city of Bosaso and sold them to cash-heavy businessmen from Mogadishu. And, because of supply and demand, the price on goods had risen dramatically.

My brief stay in Adaado was a welcome respite.

But we couldn't stay. We were running out of money, and, more importantly, Adaado had no medical facilities. If my condition worsened at all, I'd be in trouble. With a spinal cord injury, there's often a threat from all sorts of issues, from bladder infections to bedsores. Plus, we were hopeful that the peace treaty would bring what it promised: peace.

Yet again, we had to move, and we were moving back to where I didn't want to go.

We arrived back in Mogadishu in March 1992, during a time of relative peace. It was the first time I'd lived with my entire family since having been admitted to the hospital more than a year earlier. Our new residence was in the Suuqa Hoolaha (livestock market) neighborhood.

I hated it.

6 The Sacrifices of My Sisters

One year before my injury, my mother and my sister, Luul, noticed the unmistakable smell of gasoline wafting from my twenty-six-year-old sister Halima's bedroom. When they opened the door, they saw Halima engulfed in flames.

She had attempted an act rarely heard of—or, at least, rarely reported—in Somalia: suicide. For reasons unknown to us at the time, she'd doused herself in gasoline and had set herself on fire.

Thankfully, my mother and other sister threw a blanket on her as quickly as they could, dousing the fire. But Halima had seriously injured herself. Her upper chest and neck had been severely burned, with some areas having suffered third-degree burns, where even the nerve endings have been torched.

They took Halima to a nearby hospital for treatment. They would later take her in for a psychiatric evaluation, where she was diagnosed with depression. As far as I know, she hadn't told anyone about the problems she was dealing with internally because of the significant stigma that admitting to depression had in Somalia and in most developing countries. She suffered silently, reluctant to seek treatment for fear of being called a crazy person. In Somalia, a crazy person is someone who is out of control. There is no gray area. You're either a totally insane person or you're completely sane. Back then, we didn't have categories for mental illness.

So, when my spinal cord injury occurred, my parents and my sister were still recovering from that harrowing event.

To further complicate matters, my mother's second-oldest child, Luul, had a knee issue that only worsened following my accident.

So, let's take stock of what my parents were dealing with:

1. A depressed daughter who'd attempted self-immolation
2. Another daughter with a problematic knee
3. A paraplegic son
4. And, not that I would ever forget, an indiscriminate civil war.

I don't write this to garner your sympathy. These were the facts of my life, the context of our story, the backdrop for the sacrifices that my other sisters made for all of us.

Before the civil war began, my sister Ureeji was preparing to take her college entrance exam to become a teacher. When my accident occurred, my other sister, Dhuuh, was in her senior year of high school. Both Ureeji and Dhuuh were smart, talented, and resilient. They had bright futures. But just like so many hundreds if not thousands of other Somali families, they had to put off realizing their dreams for the sake of their family.

With my parents having to dedicate so much time and attention to caring for me and my older sisters struggling with their respective health issues, my middle sisters Ureeji and Dhuuh provided for us. They shouldered the financial and practical responsibilities of the household.

Ureeji, the older of the two, took the lead and established strong business connections. They sold the family shop and moved it to a larger marketplace. They began buying goods at wholesale prices from Bakarah Market, the biggest market in Mogadishu. They'd buy packages of pasta, sacks of rice, sugar, and flour, and cans of cooking oil. Ureeji would sell these items at wholesale prices at the main location while Dhuuh would sell some of the goods at retail prices in a different location, competing with local retailers. They worked effectively as a team. Ureeji would sometimes take home $250 per month. Dhuuh would take home $150. Back then—and still—that amount would make for good living. They kept our family financially stable, which would ultimately allow me the chance at a better life.

They sacrificed their young adult years for our family, a gift I can never repay.

A fragile peace existed in the city in the summer of 1992. A ceasefire, agreed to in February by the warring factions led by Ali Mehdi and General Aidiid, was still in effect. But even my thirteen-year-old self knew that such a ceasefire could cease at any moment. Conflict could erupt within a matter of hours, reversing the course of what had been months without fighting.

To complicate national matters, a severe famine was occurring in the south, particularly in the Bay and Bakol regions. The scale of the famine became apparent when video of malnourished children and adults was broadcast to the world, which was likely many viewers' first glimpse of the Somali people. According to the UN, "The magnitude of suffering was immense. Overall, an estimated 300,000 people, including many children, died. Some 2 million people, violently displaced from their home areas, fled either to neighboring countries or elsewhere within Somalia. All institutions of governance and at least 60 per cent of the country's basic infrastructure disintegrated."[6] It seemed that the severe famine was due in part to the terrible combination of the drought and the war. Aid agencies couldn't access the drought-stricken regions, and, even if they could, they feared becoming collateral damage in the still unsettled civil war.

Still, the world couldn't see those images of starving children and not act. Eventually, UN humanitarian relief agencies began providing aid to af-

---

6   "United Nations Operation in Somalia," Somalia – UNOSOM I," last modified March 21, 1997, http://www.un.org/Depts/DPKO/Missions/unosomi.htm.

fected areas. But, because of the lawlessness that abounded in those days, it was incredibly difficult for the right Somalis to secure the humanitarian supplies. Reportedly, warlords would divert and loot supply convoys before they reached their intended destinations. Additionally, these UN relief agencies would have to negotiate the politics of the warring militias who held power in the territories hardest hit by the famine. Delivering aid to those who needed it most was challenging, if not impossible.

These tragic facts led the UN Security Council to adopt Resolution 751 on April 24, 1992, which established the United Nations Operation in Somalia (UNOSOM).[7] In its official paperwork, the Council said it was "deeply disturbed by the magnitude of human suffering caused by the conflict."[8] The Council authorized 4,219 troops and fifty military observers to protect relief supplies. In August, the United States government began to airdrop relief to the Bay region. On September 14, 1992, the initial group of UN security personnel arrived in Mogadishu. In the meantime, the world continued to witness the devastation of the famine as video of severely malnourished children was constantly shown on the evening news.

I later realized that my family was a microcosm of our country. Though we were not starving like so many, we needed help, and we knew that help was not going to come from within our own country. If I were going to get better, I would have to find a way out of Somalia.

Maybe my sister Dhuuh knew that. Maybe she understood that Somalia was being torn apart by so many devastating factors that a better life was worth the risk of fleeing the country. Eventually, Dhuuh sought an opportunity to immigrate to the West. But just about any option available to a Somali citizen who wanted to leave the country during this time was

---

7   "Resolution 751," UNSCR: Search engine for the United Nations Security Council Resolutions, http://unscr.com/en/resolutions/doc/751.
8   "Resolution 751".

fraught with peril. Knowing the possible dangers, my sister still chose to travel south by road to Kenya. She reached Mombasa on August 8, 1992, where she found a relative with whom to stay.

We didn't know then how important Dhuuh's move would be for my story.

Now that she was out of the country, Dhuuh was presented with better opportunities than what had likely awaited her in Somalia. But her absence meant that the full financial responsibility of our family now fell on Ureeji's shoulders. Thankfully, Ureeji was a strong woman who knew how to navigate our chaotic city. She also relied on loyal female friends during that time, who likewise relied on her.

On December 4, 1992, a few months after Dhuuh's move, President George H. W. Bush ordered 28,000 American troops to Somalia. Their mission? To guard the humanitarian supply routes and distribution centers and ensure that the relief aid reached its intended and very needy citizens. The *New York Times* reported the president saying, "I understand the United States alone cannot right the world's wrongs, but we also know that some crises in the world cannot be resolved without American involvement, that American action is often necessary as a catalyst for broader involvement of the community of nations."[9]

A few days later, on December 9, the first US Marines landed on Mogadishu's white-sand beaches for Operation Restore Hope. The overwhelming majority of Somalis welcomed them. The world rallied behind America's leadership in support of Somalia, and more than twenty countries contributed troops to secure the supply lines. By the spring of 1993, with the help of the international community led by the United States, Somalia moved past the devastating 1992 famine.

Somalia will forever be grateful for the support it received from the

---

9   "MISSION TO SOMALIA; Bush Declares Goal in Somalia to 'Save Thousands'", The New York Times, last modified December 5, 1992, https://www.nytimes.com/1992/12/05/world/mission-to-somalia-bush-declares-goal-in-somalia-to-save-thousands.html.

United States and the international community. And, yet again, I had an early glimpse of how my life would mirror what my country had endured. In time, US intervention would play a major role in my life too.

———————

Throughout 1991 and 1992, I was mostly confined to my bed. When I wasn't in my bed, I was an astronaut. Well, I felt like I was an astronaut. To be confined to a wheelchair in Somalia during that time meant I had to prepare for my every outing as if I were an astronaut. We didn't have sidewalks, and few of our streets were even paved. Sand—my nemesis—blanketed the world around our house. Whenever I had the chance to wheel around outside, I'd inevitably sink into the sand somewhere. I quickly learned that, to get anywhere by myself, I couldn't go by myself. I'd need a copilot. Considering how often sand got stuck in one of my tire joints, I thought about "hiring" a mechanic too.

I also learned how inaccessible Somalia was to people with disabilities. Steps led into every building, with no ramps in sight. And forget about using public bathrooms. Their doors were far too narrow for anyone on a wheelchair to enter. Consequently, I didn't venture out much. It's no wonder that I stayed inside and confined to my bed for those years. The effort to become an astronaut every day was just too much. I experienced what many of my fellow civil war survivors with severe injuries did: the limitations of living in Somalia as a person with a disability prevented me from having a productive life.

I'd lay awake on my bed and wonder if I'd ever get better or if I'd ever leave Somalia. And on the truly hard days, I wondered if I'd make it to adulthood. Just as my father had been told numerous times by then, a spinal cord injury of the magnitude I suffered, in a place like this, was a death sentence. My end wouldn't arrive soon, but the difficulties of my situation would continue to deteriorate without some kind of intervention. I would slowly and painfully waste away. I didn't want that, so I focused on the positives and chose to look forward to whatever treatment my father could find for me. I have no doubt that his determination, his love, and his care for me opened wide the gates of my future.

In early 1993, he took me to a neurologist in Mogadishu who prescribed me with an injection medicine. She said that, along with physical therapy, the medicine could help regenerate some of my damaged nerves. For several weeks, I took the injection and endured physical therapy. But I didn't experience much improvement. I can't say I was surprised. They were all trying their best to offer me something that could improve my life. Still, I couldn't shake the feeling that my best hope for a brighter tomorrow lay in wait somewhere other than in Somalia.

But how in the world would my father and I ever get to anywhere else in the world?

Looking back, I should have known that it would be my sisters who would be our answer. In late 1993, Ureeji suggested that my father take me to Kenya for treatment. We could meet my sister Dhuuh, who'd just moved there a year earlier. But where would the money for our tickets to Nairobi come from? My father asked Ureeji if she had that kind of money. She nodded in the affirmative and later booked our tickets on Daallo Airlines. Then she later gave my father a thousand dollars—a lot of money back then (and still today) in Somalia. Ureeji had been taking care of us for so long, and I remain grateful for her sacrifices. Those airline tickets would change my life for the better, the answer to prayers I'd long prayed.

On Saturday, January 8, 1994, my father loaded me into the car for the drive to the airport. I remember that date because I was so sure everything would change for the better from that day forward. It did—and it didn't. My road to overcoming my significant challenges was still fraught with difficulties I couldn't foresee, like sand traps waiting to engulf my wheelchair behind every new corner.

My mother, Ureeji and her husband, Saeed, and a neighbor came along on the ride to the airport to see us off. In 1994, the Mogadishu International Airport was controlled by the United Nations. Upon our arrival at the airport, our car was stopped and searched by American soldiers. After a thorough search and checking our tickets, they allowed us to pass through. We went through the customary checking of bags, and my father and I waved our farewells to our family. We didn't know exactly how long we'd be away. And I also didn't know then that it would be the last time I'd see my sister Ureeji, at least, until we meet again in heaven, I pray.

I should have been more emotional about saying goodbye to them all, and I would have been had I'd known what my next few years would hold. But I was too excited about the possibilities for health and wellness that lay in wait for me somewhere across Somalia's borders. I was finally going to leave the place that had caused my family and me so much pain. I was anxious to leave.

That evening, my father and I arrived at Jomo Kenyatta International Airport in Nairobi, the capital city of Kenya. Dhuuh and my father's first cousin, Ali Hashi, met us at the arrival terminal. As soon as Dhuuh saw us, she sprinted toward us. After long-lasting hugs, we hailed a taxi. Fifteen minutes later, we entered the Garissa Lodge in Eastleigh Nairobi, a modest hotel with separate beds. My Aunt Amal visited us that night and provided us with a warm and delicious dinner. Our family was extremely happy that we were visiting Nairobi because they got to see us, but also because it was a much safer place than Somalia. Plus, they knew I could receive better medical treatment in their country.

My father was just as anxious to see me have relief. He asked our family, "Will there be any doctor's offices open tomorrow?"

They shook their heads no. We soon learned that Saturdays and Sundays are holidays in Kenya. This was drastically different than in Somalia, where those days were considered working days.

My father and I were both downcast to learn that I'd have to wait yet another day. Then again, it'd been almost exactly three years since my accident. I could wait another twenty-four hours.

That following Monday, on January 10, 1994, my father, my sister, and my aunt took me to a neurologist in Nairobi. He gave me a thorough examination and then announced his diagnosis: "There is no surgery that can repair Abdi's damaged spine. The damage has been done already. However, the best treatments for spinal cord injuries are in the West. I advise you try to get Abdi over there."

Like I hadn't heard that before!

My hopes for some relief in Kenya were dashed. I imagine my father was just as disappointed. But he never gave up on me. He just kept pursuing the next solution to getting his son the help he needed. My father called my brother Mustafa, who was then living in Virginia in the United States. In 1991, he'd applied to and won the diversity visa lottery, which had granted him the right to migrate to the United States. Of course, I didn't realize in 1991 how fortunate *I* would be that he'd won that lottery. Despite our twenty-five-year age gap, Mustafa was thrilled to be able to help us out.

I don't know what their conversation was like, but I imagine it was short and to the point: "Mustafa, Abdi needs more help than we can find for him in Somalia or Kenya. Could you sponsor him so he can immigrate to the states and find the help he desperately needs?"

Fortunately, my brother loved me just as much as my sisters.

7 Brace Yourself

In Nairobi, we were soon forced to move due to our dwindling resources. Since Mustafa had just begun the time-consuming process of applying to sponsor my father and me for immigration to the United States, we couldn't yet head west. So my father moved us to Mombasa, Kenya, to stay with his sister. That coastal city was three hundred miles away from Nairobi—yet another long trip with little to no accessibility along the way for people like me. Even though I was used to such trips by now, and always tried to keep my mind on our ultimate goal of getting to the US, it was still a hard journey.

A few days after we were settled, my father took me to the Mombasa General Hospital. We waited for two hours to see a doctor. He reviewed a sore on my lower back that had been bothering me for months. I hadn't been able to sit for long periods of time because of the placement of the sore. And every time I tried to sit, it felt like the wound was just getting worse. The doctor prescribed an antibiotic for me, but he also gave me something even more useful: he suggested that I should start using leg braces.

As a fifteen-year-old, I'd never heard of such things. I thought that only amputees were given new legs. I didn't know the difference between prosthetic legs and leg braces. The doctor must have been able to see the incredulity on my face, so he patiently explained what leg braces could do for me. "You'll be able to walk outside, with some assistance, of course."

My eyes went even wider. That was all I needed to hear. I wanted leg braces—immediately. I could tell by the look on my father's face that he was likewise just as excited about the possibilities. The doctor scheduled us for a follow-up appointment at an orthopedic clinic.

A few days later, a clinician measured my height and my feet, then told us to return in a couple of weeks. Those two weeks I had to wait were filled with dreams of what could be. *With these braces and two walking sticks, I'll be able to breathe the fresh, breezy air of a coastal Mombasa morning. I'll be able to walk—walk!—in the cool of the afternoon, once the sun has started its descent.* I told my father about these dreams. He'd just smile in reply.

Filled with hopeful anticipation, we returned to the orthopedic clinic. The physical therapist brought out *my* leg braces. Without hesitation, I allowed him to place the braces on my legs and tie up the straps that would hold them in place. The therapist lifted me up for my first time to walk since my accident three years earlier.

I wobbled with my first few steps, but the therapist reassured me that I wouldn't fall down. After several trials, I became more comfortable—so long as I used someone else for extra support. The therapist showed my father, if he thought I was really going to fall, how to grab my belt. As the therapist saw us both grasping this new reality and smiling all the way through, he released us.

We went home genuinely excited. My father even joked, "Maybe you won't need me anymore. The braces might be your wings now, to let you fly again, like a bird freed from a cage, to breathe the fresh air of freedom and go do whatever you wish." I couldn't wait to stretch my wings the next day.

But this bird still had to realize his limitations. It didn't take me long to understand that, due to the limited control I had of my balance, it'd be hard for me to venture out on my own, even with my leg braces. I would always need someone standing next to me or behind me to keep me from eventually falling over. The therapist who'd told me I wouldn't fall over likely hadn't known the full extent of my injuries. I didn't blame him for those words. After all, he had given me the gift of at least being able to walk upright, even if I still needed others' help. That was more hope than so many other doctors had given me over the years.

I put those leg braces on every morning and every afternoon to venture outside of my house. I didn't go far, but it was still something new and different and wonderful. Most of the time, I'd walk just a bit and then sit outside. Across the street from the house in which we were living sat another house with a nice concrete balcony facing the eastern sky. My cousins, friends, and I would often sit on that balcony until sunset, drinking tea, making jokes, laughing at each other, and sharing our dreams and aspirations.

As I enjoyed those rare moments of hopeful calmness on that balcony, much was changing with our family. My sister Dhuuh married a man in Switzerland through an arranged marriage in the fall of 1994. Her husband-to-be had sent her travel documents. Within a few weeks of receiving them, she'd flown to Rome and then taken a train to Geneva, Switzerland. Hearing about how quickly she'd gotten out of Kenya made me wonder if my father and I could get to Europe just as easily.

In those days, it seemed as if the only talk in our town was about who was getting to Europe, the US, or Canada. Every Somali refugee appeared desperate to leave Kenya. That was also when the first waves of Somali refugees began pouring into America. They likewise wanted the better opportunities that the West seemed to offer. Apparently, I was one of many who believed that my hopeful future lay in wait somewhere beyond the Atlantic.

Dhuuh's quick departure to Europe left my father and me in need of help with daily responsibilities like cooking and cleaning. My father, who always seemed to have a contingency plan in place, asked my older sister, Luul, to join us in Mombasa. Even though she was dealing with a knee problem that had plagued her for more than a decade, she said yes and joined us. Again, another sister was giving of her time to care for me, and I will always remain grateful to her for showing me such love.

In late 1994, my father found love in Mombasa. I was thrilled for him, knowing that he had suffered alongside me for so long and had sacrificed so much of his time for my care. This new love obviously reenergized him and gave him even more hope for his future. While at a Mombasa shopping market, my father met Halima Gedi, a Kenyan citizen of Somali descent. After their first meeting, he kept visiting her, and soon thereafter he proposed to her. She quickly agreed, and they were married in quick succession.

This meant I had to move out of the room at our house that my father and I had shared and into the living room. But I was glad to do so. I wanted my father to be happy, and I could easily tell that he was. Plus, our relatively big house had a spacious living room. Some of my cousins would sleep there from time to time, so I was excited to join their group.

I believe some people who knew my father's new wife were surprised that she would marry an older man who was also a Somali refugee with a disabled son. Maybe they thought that she saw an opportunity to get to America through us. If that was the case, could I blame her? That's where we all wanted to get to. But I don't think it was. They seemed to genuinely love and care for one another.

After a couple of months at our house, Halima chose to visit her mother in Garissa, Kenya, a trip that would require at least seven hours on the road. She stayed there for several weeks. While she was there, our screening interview was posted on the Utanga Refugee bulletin board. From what we could ascertain through rumors, the Embassy only scheduled screening interviews every few months, so we were ecstatic that we wouldn't have to wait much longer.

The interview was a face-to-face meeting that my father and I both attended. I distinctly remember speaking with Pam, a soft-spoken, pleasant woman who seemed to have interviewed dozens of refugees like me. She was so well-known and liked by the other refugees that they had even joked about her knowledge of their tribes and strongholds. She asked us basic questions: "What city did you come from? How long have you been in Kenya? What happened to Abdi?" We gave her our story one answer at a time.

We completed that interview, the first of many steps toward immigrating. Then we were told to prepare for the full interview, which would take place, of course, back in Nairobi—three hundred miles away.

———————

The evening buses that shuttled riders from Mombasa to Nairobi typically left Mombasa at 9 p.m. and would arrive in Nairobi the next morning at 5 a.m. They would only make one stop for food and a bathroom break. To add to this inconvenience, these buses had no wheelchair-accessible ramps or accommodations. (They may still be that way!) My father and a cousin would have to pick me up from my wheelchair and walk me to my seat—quite an unpleasant experience. (It was too difficult to use my leg braces on the steps leading into those buses, but we did have them stowed in our luggage.)

To be blunt, I hated these long bus trips.

But this ride was different.

I was actually *enthusiastic* about leaving. As we pulled out of the bus station in Mombasa, I kept looking back at the city, thinking and hoping it would be the last time I'd see that place. I wanted it to be my final goodbye because I was on my way to America.

By the time we arrived in Nairobi, right at 5 a.m. the next morning, I was exhausted. We waited for dawn to break, and my father hailed a taxi to take us to the Garissa Lodge in Eastleigh, Nairobi. We booked a first-floor room and recuperated from our long trip.

The next day, we headed to the US Embassy in Nairobi to inquire about our next steps for immigrating. An embassy staffer, a blonde woman in her thirties, told us that our interview would take place in Ifo, a refugee camp near the border of Kenya and Somalia.

We were shocked, and not just because the new location would require further travel. Ifo was so close to the border that it presented a legitimate security threat. After all our travels, for thousands of miles back and forth, they were going to send us back into the belly of the beast—or at least close enough to where we'd be dessert if the beast's hunger wasn't sated by what it could find in its homeland.

My father pleaded with the embassy staffer for some alternative location. He pointed out my readily apparent condition and the lack of any medical facility in Ifo.

His pleas fell on deaf ears. She immediately denied our request for another location. This woman whom I'd thought a beauty, partially because she was the first real symbol of my possible immigration to the US, had turned into a beast. She had basically told us that we *had* to go to Ifo or forfeit any hope for immigration.

Back at our hotel, I let my emotions out. "Father, I can't go to Ifo. I don't want to die there. All those things we've been hearing about the horrible conditions in Ifo? We can't risk it. Let our process die here." I was devastated and demoralized. I had experienced disappointment before, but this time was different. I felt that my hopes for a better future had been decimated. I thought, *After all we've endured and all we've done—all my* dad *has done—this is what we get!?*

But my father would hear nothing of giving up. That wasn't his nature, and I'm incredibly grateful for his tenacity in the face of setback after setback. He called his sister, the same aunt we'd stayed with in Mombasa. She was actually in the process of immigrating to the US too, and she'd already moved to Ifo. She related that the place was harsh but livable. Still, she admitted to being concerned about me having to live in a place like that.

But, as had always been the case, no matter where we were in the world or the uphill battles we were facing, my father chose to put his trust in God.

"Abdi, we're going to Ifo. If we don't, our only alternative is going back to Somalia, and that's hell on earth."

I composed myself, nodded, and braced myself for Ifo.

We left Nairobi on Thursday, January 26, 1995, and reached Garissa, where we stayed the night. The next morning, we took another bus to the Ifo refugee camp, about seventy miles northeast but at least two-and-a-half hours of yet another bumpy bus ride. We arrived in Ifo around 1 p.m. and discovered firsthand exactly what my father had told the embassy staffer just two days earlier: it was *hot*.

The only relief in sight was the one restaurant I saw with a lone generator connected to a small refrigerator. Their water was at least almost cold. Otherwise, I saw no air conditioners or fans. Now, I'd never had air conditioning anywhere else, but the temperatures in Mombasa, Nairobi, and Mogadishu were at least tolerable, in the mid-to-upper nineties. But Ifo's temperature often soared to over one hundred degrees, and, of course, we'd arrived at the hottest period of the year. The heat was even more unbearable considering we'd live in a tent rather than a brick structure. And it didn't seem as though you could even buy ice anywhere. Maybe these were comforts I had taken for granted. Then I had to remind myself that we were at a refugee camp. Such simple niceties as ice would be seen as luxuries. Even though I hadn't been there long, my skin felt as if it were becoming drier and darker by the second. The heat was unbearable, and the knowledge that no relief was forthcoming made it even more so.

Ifo was populated by maybe hundreds of thousands of refugees, a majority of whom were likely Somalis displaced by our civil war. The looks on every man, woman, and child told me that they weren't concerned with where to find ice. They needed food, water, medicine, and shelter.

I thought I had been prepared for Ifo. I had thought wrong. My fears about dying in Ifo roared back to life at seeing the condition of the place. *If seemingly healthy people were in such bad shape, what hope do I have?* But even in my anxiety, my father's comforting words would come to mind: "Trust God, Abdi."

My aunt greeted us at Ifo, and then my father sought a location for our tent. A kind family—coincidentally from the Adaado area—offered us a spot near them. We pitched our camp and tried to make the best of an absurd situation. The cackling hyenas at night did little to calm my nerves. Plus, we fasted for the holy month of Ramadan as it fell in February of that year. To say the least, it was difficult for me to adjust to this new environment.

Still, I wanted to be positive. Even though our surroundings seemed dire, this was the closest we'd been to getting West. I felt that if only I could endure this hardship for a few more weeks, maybe our goal of immigrating to the US will come to fruition. It would seem such a waste if we were to give up now. So I chose to be optimistic and tried to adapt to Ifo.

One bright spot was the multinational soccer tournament. Teams representing Somalia, Kenya, Ethiopia, and South Sudan would play on a field near our tent in the late afternoon, when the temperature was only mildly hot and not searing. I recall that the South Sudanese team was particularly tall, strong, and skillful. Our Somali team was skilled too, but they were no match for the South Sudanese. Still, I cheered for my homeland.

Of course, my main source of inspiration was the same as most everyone else within the camp: checking the interview list at the front of the United Nations office every weekday morning. Once our names got on that list, I knew it wouldn't be long before we'd be on a plane, leaving Ifo, Nairobi, Mombasa, Mogadishu, and my disability behind.

We didn't see our names on that list until May 1995, four months after our arrival in Ifo.

8 Yearning to Breathe Free

When it comes to immigration, no process is fast. That said, I was still surprised at the relatively quick series of events that transpired after my father spotted our names on that coveted list outside the U.N. office in Ifo in early May of 1995.

After completing the interview, the results were posted on that same bulletin board a few days later. We'd passed! Our momentary celebration was cut short by the realization that the next step of the process was—yet again—three hundred miles away, back in Nairobi. By this point, it felt as if traveling to Nairobi were my full-time job.

One harrowing event took place on our bumpy bus ride to Nairobi. Security guards stopped us at a checkpoint in Garissa. I saw people from the bus in front of us, which had also been traveling from Ifo, being refused entry. They sulked past our bus, forced to walk back to Ifo or wherever they could find a place to stay in Garissa that night. I felt bad for them for a moment, but I feared the same could happen to us. Again, to have come this far? To have finally been chosen for our interview and to have passed, only to be turned back now, still stuck in Kenya, never to get to the U.S., where I knew my life and health could be better? Every fear I'd had over the last few years came roaring back into my conscious mind as I watched these rejected men and women shuffle by.

My father asked another person on the bus about what was happening.

"They're turning back riders who don't have their refugee card or Kenyan residence card. Hope you have your papers." The man paused and looked ahead. "But it seems they're letting some people through without their cards."

In other words, some passengers were being allowed to enter because they'd bribed the guards.

Once it was our turn to go through the checkpoint, my father showed our Ifo refugee papers. We were allowed to pass through. As soon as our bus was cleared, I hoped that the driver would accelerate as fast as possible. I wanted to be as far away from rejection as I could.

Seven hours later, we arrived in Nairobi. The next morning, we thoroughly reviewed the papers we'd received from the interviewing staff at Ifo. They had specific instructions about our next steps to ensure our immigration. I would have to undergo a full medical screening at a specific location in Nairobi, so we traveled to a doctor's office near downtown, where they gave us a date for my screening. Two or three days later, they X-rayed me and drew my blood. A copy of my screening results was sent to the US Embassy in Nairobi. We anxiously awaited the results as well. A few diseases, like HIV, would automatically disqualify someone from immigration. I had no reason to fear failing these tests, but, given everything I'd experienced up to that point, I was still nervous. I knew that our progress toward getting to the US could be derailed by even the smallest of issues—like a drop of blood.

In June of 1995, we received confirmation from the embassy that I'd passed my screening. We were told to wait for our visas and travel packages, which included our Gulf Air tickets, our I-94 cards (the US "Arrival-Departure Record Card"), and a yellow sealed envelope that we were directed not to open. This envelope was to be given to US immigration officials at our first appointment. I could only assume that it contained our immigration papers and records. While all of this was occurring, my brother Mustafa had rented a two-bedroom apartment for us in Alexandria, Virginia.

In July of 1995, we received our visas and our airfare.

On August 22, 1995, we departed Jomo Kenyatta International Airport in Nairobi, Kenya.

On August 23, 1995, against a clear blue sky, I saw New York City's inimitable skyline from the air. Lady Liberty welcomed us to our new home. We landed at JFK, where I distinctly remember the politeness of the airline employees as they helped me off the plane and to our next gate. A short flight later, we landed at Dulles International Airport near Washington, D.C.

It was the happiest moment of all my sixteen years of living, the realization of a dream I'd always feared would never come true.

We checked into the customs office at Dulles. While they reviewed our papers, they asked, "Are you excited to be the newest immigrants to the US?"

Our faces should have told them enough, but we excitedly answered, "Yes, yes!"

Seeing that our papers were in order, we were officially welcomed into the country. Then we headed to get our bags, where we immediately saw Mustafa. His grin was just as large as ours. We hugged for too long, gathered our luggage, then got into Mustafa's car. During the drive, I imagine my eyes were wide and my mouth wide open as I stared at the landscape blurring by. The highways, the bridges, the *pavement*! Of the thousands of thoughts that coursed through my mind during that "bumpless" ride, I suddenly realized, *No sand anywhere!*

My mind kept getting ahead of itself: *Could it be that every hope I'd had in Somalia and Kenya about what living in the US would be like could be true? Will I be able to finally be independent? Will I see improvement in my condition? Will I be able to walk on my own feet again? Is a miracle cure awaiting me?* My expectations were soaring.

We arrived at our new apartment in Alexandria, Virginia, dropped off our luggage, then went to a cousin's apartment, where we enjoyed a home-cooked family meal. The aunt with whom we'd stayed in Mombasa was also there. We devoured the food. We talked about Kenya. We laughed with each other. And, maybe most importantly in hindsight, the family members who'd been living in the US for a time leveled our expectations. From their own experiences of being immigrants to this country from Somalia, they knew what was coursing through our minds. They knew the pictures we were likely imagining were farfetched. I imagine they worried even more about what I thought would be possible. So they tried to tell us as best they could what living in America was really like. They didn't want our high expectations to ultimately crush us.

Which was a good choice on their part. After waiting for so long just to get on American soil, I thought all of my problems would be magically fixed in *maybe* a few months.

I couldn't have known then that my struggles would continue. They'd just be different than they were before. But, at least America has no sand. Fortunately, the Americans with Disabilities Act was signed into law by President George H. W. Bush in 1990, which mandated equal access under the law.

I'm still grateful for those facts.

We couldn't learn of my next medical steps until Medicaid covered my expenses, which required about a month of impatient waiting. Even though my mind was centered on seeking a cure for my spinal injury, I knew nothing could be done until that next medical appointment. During that time, I tried to acclimate myself to my new and very different surroundings. I learned as much as I could from my family. My cousins spoke of finding a job, buying cars, and planning their respective futures. Their collective optimism seemed to fill the air, and I couldn't wait to breathe that same free air. In addition to healing, I wanted a job, a car, and a future. The US seemed to promise it all.

Of course, the choices that America offered were best symbolized by its malls and grocery stores. I was mesmerized by them. I never knew one item could have so many different variants. For instance, the going joke within the Somali immigrant community was, "Don't get confused by the dog food," meaning that our inexperience in shopping with so many choices could lead us to mistake dog food for human food.

Mostly, I hung out with family and other Somali immigrants. I tried to glean as much as I could about what it would require of me to live and thrive in this place. And I remember much laughter. One time, memorably, when our group had gotten too loud, a white American woman knocked on our door. My sister Luul opened the door. The woman screamed, "We can't sleep, so shut the **** up!"

None of us knew that word, so none of us were offended.

Finally, on September 23, 1995, I was admitted to Inova Alexandria Hospital. In addition to reviewing my case, they treated a small open wound on my lower back that had been bothering me for quite some time. But, without intending to, they opened a deeper wound within me.

Like too many before him, the doctor who'd reviewed me gave me another prognosis I didn't want to hear. "I'm sorry, Abdi. There's nothing we can do for your spinal cord injury due to its severity. If your injury had occurred *in the US* and you would have sought specialized help *within twenty-four hours* of the injury, you *might* have had a *small* chance for recovery."

I felt like he was emphasizing those certain words to help me feel better, as if my misfortune of being in the wrong place at the wrong time is what had prevented me from one day being fully healed. Or that, even if I'd been hurt in America, the chances of a full recovery were still slim.

But I was sixteen. All I really heard was, "We can't help you. You're broken."

At that point, I thought of my dad's resilience—how he'd never relent even in the face of insurmountable odds. When given an outcome he didn't want, he wouldn't complain. He'd just find another way.

I realized the doctor was still speaking to me. "Could you repeat what you just said?"

"There's nothing we can do for your injury, Abdi."

"So why am I here? Why did I come all this way to seek help it looks like you can't give me?"

The doctor nodded his head in understanding. "I understand, Abdi. There's nothing we can do for your injury, but there's much *you* can do for your injury."

I knew where he was going with this, but I let him keep talking.

"Your only option is rigorous physical therapy."

I was right.

"With the right help, and if you really apply yourself, you can relearn how to live independently. You can learn how to transfer yourself into and out of your bed and your wheelchair. You can use the restroom by yourself, take a shower by yourself, use the kitchen by yourself, and go outside by yourself. No help necessary."

I smiled on the outside. What sixteen-year-old—and especially one who'd been confined to a wheelchair—*didn't* long for freedom and independence? But that smile betrayed how I truly felt.

My family may have tempered my expectations, but this doctor had just crushed them.

———————

On January 4, 1996, my father clutched his chest in pain. I called 911 and rode in the ambulance with my father to the emergency room. All I could think during that ride was how much I loved my father. He meant the world to me twice over. I feared what would happen to me should anything happen to him. I tried to push those thoughts away, but the reality of our situation—the blare of the siren, us speeding down the highway, my father barely breathing—was all too real. I couldn't help but consider my father's mortality.

At the ER, I was my father's de facto translator. After a few tests, the doctors discovered that he'd *only* had chest pains. No heart attack or other intense issues. We were sent home, and the doctors had recommended that my father begin exercising more regularly.

A few months later, on August 22, 1996, almost a year to the day since our arrival in the US, my father underwent an angioplasty to open a blocked coronary artery. He stayed at the hospital for a few days and fully recovered a week later.

From that first 911 call to his arrival home after his heart procedure, this kind of thought often crossed my mind: *Be thankful for the opportunity to pursue independence. Someday, you may not have the help you've always leaned on.*

On February 6, 1996, about a month after my father's chest pains first started, I began physical therapy at Inova Mount Vernon Hospital in Alexandria. I endured five rigorous therapy sessions per week for three months. Each session lasted between thirty and forty-five minutes. We worked on building my lower body strength, reducing spasms, and how I could live independently. Every minute seemed as grueling as the one that preceded it.

Inova was a full-time, inpatient care facility, which meant I stayed on campus morning, noon, and night. To be blunt, I hated it. I didn't like being away from my family. I didn't like what I felt I was being forced to do. I didn't like more pain. But, most of all, I didn't like the constant reminder that this was apparently the best it was ever going to get. In other words, the harsh reality that I'd likely never walk again was truly settling in. Every labored effort I took in physical therapy was yet another reminder that I was very likely going to spend the rest of my life using a wheelchair. All the hopes I'd placed in coming to America were being dashed one hour at a time. I felt as if my world were upside down because it wasn't what I'd expected, and far less than what I'd dreamed. After dreaming for so long about what the US could provide to me, I didn't want to face the truth of my situation.

To frustrate my teenage self further, I was the only young person there. Everywhere I looked, I saw senior adults going through the same kinds of arduous physical therapy I was enduring, except they were often moving much slower. I had no one to talk to, and I'm certain this fact contributed to my bleak, joyless outlook on my future. But at least the hospital offered a movie night once a week. That was often my high point—until another paraplegic close to my age showed up.

As the representative of a mobility company, this young man visited one of our therapy sessions to talk about his company. He seemed to be in his mid-twenties, well-dressed, and looked like a full-time professional— even as a paraplegic. Back then, especially as I was warring against myself and my likely future confined to a wheelchair, I'd never met someone like him. Even his appearance gave me hope.

Despite my language limitations—I used a combination of hand gestures and short words—we chatted for a few minutes. I just had to know more about his job and his life.

I asked, "Who brought you to the hospital?"

With a smile, he replied, "I drove myself."

I didn't believe him. I thought he was joking, so I pressed further. "Show me."

With his grin widening, he said, "Of course. Give me a few minutes and I'll bring my car to the front entrance." The man wheeled out.

I waited rather impatiently, my thoughts racing about the possibilities—if he were telling me the truth.

He returned soon enough. "Do you still want to see it?"

With a beaming smile, I exclaimed, "Yes, yes!"

We rolled to the front entrance and out the door. His decade-old, two-door sedan wasn't much to look at, but it would soon become the most amazing car I'd ever seen.

As he wheeled down to the driver's side door, he glanced behind himself and made eye contact with me. "Watch."

As if I could do anything else.

He opened the driver's side door. The man effortlessly slid from his wheelchair and into the driver's seat. In a fluid motion that was obviously the result of constant practice, he grabbed his wheelchair, removed its wheels, folded the chair, and stashed it in his back seat. Then he closed his door. The seemingly complicated process had taken just a few seconds, but I felt like I'd watched him in slow motion. My eyes went wide. I thought, *What magic! What possibilities!*

He reversed the process and extricated himself from his car, smiling all the time. By the surprised look on my face, he must have known what was going on in my mind. He wheeled beside me, knowing I was about to burst with more questions.

After talking more about driving, I asked him a bigger question, one I'd been wrestling with for a long time and that encapsulated my fears about becoming an adult paraplegic: "How do you live?" I shared how I didn't want to be cared for for the rest of my life, how I wanted to venture out into the world on my own.

He nodded his head. "I understand completely. How do I live? I live in an apartment—by myself."

Part of me still couldn't believe what he was telling me. I'd been living with and essentially relying on other people at all times ever since my accident.

We spoke at length on that beautiful day, and that young man provided me with an unambiguous roadmap of possibilities. He reignited my ashen hopes. He breathed life into my dying dreams. He clarified my future. As he slid into his car one last time and waved goodbye, I knew I'd caught a glimpse of my future self.

A few days after that chance encounter, I was discharged and went home. Even though I was disheartened by much of my experience at therapy, I tried to make the best of it. During those three months, I'd been trained on simple but necessary tasks for regaining my independence, like how to transfer myself into and out of my wheelchair and how to maneuver my wheelchair more easily.

Though I was grateful to have learned those skills, there was only one new skill I was legitimately excited about.

"Dad! I can drive! I saw a man just like me, driving by himself. He showed me!"

He didn't believe me, but I didn't relent. The longer I spoke about it, the more he believed. He knew my determination to succeed. After all, I'd learned it from him.

9 Driven to Succeed

We moved to Raleigh, North Carolina, in October 1996. I enrolled at Athens Drive High School as a freshman. Most everyone's freshman year is daunting because of how momentous a change it can be. I had the same anxieties about entering high school, but they were compounded by three rather significant differences from a majority of my classmates: I was in a wheelchair, I had recently immigrated from a foreign country, and I still struggled with English. I knew my first full year of education in America would be an uphill battle.

Then again, my life since my accident had been that way. And my father, my family, and I had fought—and won—every battle within our control since then. I knew I could overcome these challenges, but I also knew that much would be asked of me. My future depended on me excelling in education. If I wasn't successful in school, my only alternative was becoming a welfare recipient, and that was unimaginable to me. That's why, given the fact that I was paralyzed from the waist down and operating at half capacity compared to my peers, I made a conscious effort to work twice as hard as anyone else. My obstacles to success may have loomed large, but I never doubted my will to succeed.

For the first few months, I rode the school bus—until the day I said, "I can drive." Mustafa and a cousin then challenged me to put my wheelchair into Mustafa's car. I quickly retorted that I could, in fact, drive a car. They laughed and said, "Prove us wrong!"

Their faces looked just like mine back at physical therapy, when the young professional in a wheelchair had told me *he* could drive. They didn't believe me. In fact, they bet me a hundred dollars that I couldn't even get myself and my wheelchair into Mustafa's four-door sedan unassisted.

I took their bet on the spot. "Let's do it right now!"

We went outside to Mustafa's car. I opened the driver's side door, edged my wheelchair close to the driver's seat, put my feet on the ground, and inched closer to the seat within the car. I placed my left hand on my wheelchair and set my right hand on the driver's seat. Without assistance, I pulled myself onto the driver's seat. Then I removed the wheels from my wheelchair, folded the wheelchair, and placed it in the front passenger's seat. I wasn't as fluid as that young professional, but only I knew that. I still needed to practice more!

But my brother and my cousin were stunned—and particularly my brother, who'd made the bet.

I let him off the hook. "I don't need your hundred dollars, but I need something bigger. I need a car."

After telling this story to my dad, he finally realized I was ready to drive myself. He may have also thought how helpful it would be for me to transport myself everywhere. And he likely knew how important it would be to my mental and emotional health to have that kind of independence. Or, because I'd been talking about driving and getting my car for so long, maybe he just relented. Soon enough, my father, my brother, and I were shopping for a two-door car. I emphasized to them that I preferred two-door models because they had wider doors, which gave me more room to maneuver my wheelchair in and out.

As we searched for the right car, I meticulously read a driver's license booklet. I wanted to ace my test and get into my own car as quickly as possible. But I failed the written portion of my first test! I couldn't believe it, but I wasn't terribly discouraged. I became even more determined to get my license. On my second attempt, I passed the written portion.

A few weeks later, we bought my first car: a 1994 Geo Metro. We took it to a mobility shop nearby where they installed hand control equipment that would allow me to use the gas and brake pedals with my hands. They showed me how to use the hand control equipment as well.

I had seldom been so ready to be free.

Mustafa rode along with me around the streets of Raleigh as I kept preparing for my first driving test. Once I felt ready, we went to the DMV for my driving test—which I failed! When I asked the instructor why, he replied that I'd failed to look over my shoulder while making a right turn. I was downtrodden. Would I ever get my license?

A few days later, I took the driving test for the second time. Finally, I passed the driving test. The day I received my driver's license was an incredibly momentous day. That small piece of plastic symbolized much more than just a teenager getting a car; it was my passport to independence.

Not only would I be able to drive myself to and from school and medical appointments, but I could also take my father and sisters to the grocery store, or to the mosque, or to *their* medical appointments. No longer would I be a drain on my family's time. I could contribute! As an active kid who wanted to do more for my family, I was enthusiastic about the possibilities. It felt like untapped energies were just beginning to gush out.

My car gifted me with newfound freedoms. I was no longer restricted to my home. I was a bird finally freed from its nest. I could hang out with my friends *without* having to ask for a ride to wherever they were. I could drive to see them at the mosque, in a shopping center, or at the coffee shop we enjoyed. What once had seemed far out of reach and out of range for me became *normal*. I regained a piece of freedom most people don't even realize they have.

Another benefit that car ownership and state-certified licensure brought was the freedom of time it granted me. Before having my own car, I was always constrained by other people's time, always dependent on everyone else's schedules. I had to be. But, with a car, I could better dictate my own schedule. This was the most helpful when it came to my English as a Second Language (ESL) tutoring.

On top of starting a new school, entering high school, being in a wheelchair, and being from a foreign country, I also had to *learn English* as I attended school.

Like I said: I had to work twice as hard. I'm not complaining about it, though. I never wanted whatever the alternative might have been. I wanted what was at the end of all that hard work: health, happiness, and success in America.

So I did my best to excel in all of my classes, and I knew that ESL tutoring was the essential class to help me do so. I would receive ESL tutoring throughout my high school years. While my first year at Athens Drive had gone as well as I could expect, I floundered in my second year. I got a D in my English Literature class, meaning I'd have to retake the class—and I did not want to spend another year taking that class.

Fortunately, I learned that the school was offering a fast-paced version of that class the following summer. But school counselors advised me against taking it, fearing that the fast pace—essays had to be written and returned in quick succession—would be too challenging for someone still learning the language.

Having heard people doubt me all my life, the only part of their advisement I considered was that I might need more help to get through the class. So I inquired about getting assistance from one of my ESL instructors. Unfortunately, no ESL classes would be offered that summer, and no ESL instructors would even be working.

That's when Mary Mason saved my educational life. During tutoring one day prior to that summer, I shared my dilemma with her. She graciously offered to assist me, meaning that she'd come to the school every weekday afternoon that summer just to help me. She would sacrifice her summer for me. To this day, I still find her generosity hard to believe, and I remain grateful to her.

Prior to agreeing, she told me, "As long as you can promise me of your one-hundred percent commitment to succeed, then I will be there to help you."

I replied, "I will promise you one-hundred-and-fifty percent."

She laughed and agreed to our summer arrangement.

During the summer of 1998, I attended English Literature from 8 a.m. to noon every Monday through Friday. After a quick lunch break, I'd meet Mrs. Mason in the school's library. With her language assistance, I'd write my essays about *The Scarlet Letter, Macbeth, The Crucible,* or *To Kill a Mockingbird,* print them in the library, and then turn them in the next day. And, because I could drive myself, we would sometimes stay there until 3 or 4 p.m. The freedom of my car, which meant the freedom of my time, gave me the freedom to put 150 percent of myself into my studies.

Thanks to Mrs. Mason's tremendous sacrifice, I received a B+ for my efforts. The school deleted my D. The successful conclusion to that significant challenge proved to me that, with the right help, anything was possible if I could also commit to giving 100—or 150—percent. I'd seen my blueprint for future success: hard work plus determination, with a bit of help, makes for endless possibilities. From that point on, I never doubted what I was capable of accomplishing.

After overcoming the challenge of my sophomore-year English Lit class, nothing else in high school seemed as daunting. I enjoyed my junior year—maybe because I was finally able to give serious consideration to life after high school. For a time, I thought about enrolling in computer programming courses for up to a year and becoming certified in a certain programming language. But I knew that continuing my education was essential to my future success in life, which meant I had to begin researching colleges. I wanted a four-year degree.

But, just like the other motivated students in my class, I had to keep my chief focus on finishing school well so that I could attend the university of my choice. With gratitude to all of my teachers—and particularly Mrs. Mason—I did well in high school. In fact, I was locally recognized for my hard work despite my apparent barriers to success. In the spring of

2000, I received the "Spotlight on Students: An Award for Outstanding Achievement" from the Wake County Public School System. The coveted award for exceeding above and beyond in the face of extreme adversity had been broadcast on the local news in Raleigh. The next day, I was a minor celebrity, receiving high-fives and greetings from friends, and even people I didn't know, who'd watched the award ceremony on the local news channels.

I graduated high school in May of 2000. I will never forget the beaming smile of pride that arced across my father's face as I rolled across the stage to receive my diploma. Just five years prior, when we had first immigrated to the United States, I'm not sure either of us could have seen this day coming. Sure, we had hoped for it, but, given my health condition and the many other obstacles stacked against us, such a normal dream of graduating high school seemed far out of our reach.

I couldn't help but wonder if I were dreaming—but the paper in my hand proved to me this dream was real.

10 American Misunderstandings

Even though I'd been in the country for six years, I still had much to learn. One hilarious moment from the spring of 2001 stands out. The internet at our apartment wasn't working, so I called for a technician. After I let him in, he asked about the problem.

I replied, "I'm getting a sporadic connection through my phone jack."

"Hmm. Let me check the landline connection outside." The technician casually walked back outside. A few minutes later, he rushed back in. He seemed frightened.

I couldn't help but ask, "What happened?"

"Oh man! I was almost killed by a black widow!"

I'd never heard that phrase before.

He continued, "It came so close. She almost bit me! And she was really big."

I thought, *What did you do to get such a reaction from my black neighbor?* But all I said was, "What did you do?"

"I was pulling the cable underneath some bushes out there and she suddenly jumped out at me!"

I thought, *She jumped at you? Really? That's crazy!* But all I said was, "What did you do next?"

"I ran out. She almost got me!"

My next series of thoughts tried to make sense of what I was hearing. *I know my neighbor. She's not violent. But maybe this guy pulled the cable too hard and ripped her phone jack out? Maybe that's what angered her so much? But what was she doing in the bushes in the first place?*

The more I thought about what the technician was telling me, the more bizarre the scenario became. We were both laughing by this point. Not knowing what to say or do, I asked the technician, "Well, do you want me to talk to her?"

The technician looked at me strangely. "How're you gonna do that?"

"I'll just knock on her door."

Then he really started laughing. He'd realized I didn't know what a black widow was. Well, at least a black widow spider. "No, no, no! That's not what I meant. A black widow is a type of spider. That's what I saw in the bushes."

The proverbial light came on above my head. "Oh! That makes so much more sense."

We laughed even more. He fixed my internet issue. And I will always remember what a black widow spider is.

That experience was just one of many that constantly reminded me I still had more to learn about living in America.

The year before that incident, in August 2000, I'd enrolled at Wake Technical Community College to earn my associate degree. Every weekday morning, I drove my red, two-door Geo Metro 11.3 miles to the Wake Tech campus southeast of Raleigh, anxious to learn.

Knowing that I had to keep a GPA of 3.0 or higher in order to graduate, I was strategic about my choice of classes. During my first year, I took a few prerequisite courses to shore up my knowledge gaps in English and Math. I also never took two math courses or two science courses in the same semester because I wanted to avoid risking downgrading my 3.0 GPA. I made sure to take advantage of the student resources available at the International Students' Center, where I'd work on my essays and get assistance with writing and editing as well as math. I would often complete most if not all of my homework at the center before heading home.

When my father and I would talk about my career aspirations—if my health improved enough—he always pushed me toward working in hospitals as a nurse or nursing assistant. I didn't picture myself in a nurse's gown. I didn't know any male or female nurses in my community, and I'd never seen a nurse in a wheelchair in real life—or on TV.

I was always interested to find out the newest upward career trajectory by periodically checking with my college advisors. They spoke about computers. The thought of earning a degree in computing compelled me, at least conceptually. But I knew I'd have to work very hard to get into a computer major. My first goal was to do well during my two years of college.

––––––––––––––

On another memorable morning during my college years, I vividly remember eating breakfast while watching *The Today Show* with my father and sister, Luul. Then "BREAKING NEWS" flashed across the screen and the world changed forever.

What we saw next didn't make sense. It couldn't be possible. Flying planes into buildings?

I sat transfixed, spellbound by the images, but I had to get to my sociology class. I left home distressed only to get to Wake Tech and find every student and teacher huddled around the television in the library. Looking at the faces around me, the magnitude of the day's shock and grief sank in. The more I thought about what was happening, the more anxious I became.

Especially when the attackers were identified as Muslims.

In the weeks and months that followed, some media outlets used the tragedy of 9/11 to cast doubt on the entire Muslim community. Not only did they question our religion, they also questioned our loyalty to the country. For the first time I could remember, I was conflicted about the country that had adopted me. Immigrating to America had opened all kinds of doors of opportunity for me. Most every American I'd met since arriving had welcomed me and my family with open arms. The kindness, hospitality, and generosity we'd experienced since 1995 cannot be overstated.

We were shaken by the 9/11 attacks. Every person I knew in my community had the same questions: How could Muslims have killed nearly three thousand innocent people, including other Muslims? We were all shocked, but evil knows no religion, race, or ethnicity. The 9/11 perpetrators fit the same category as those men who had destroyed Somalia and who had killed countless thousands of innocent people.

In the months following September 11th, American Muslims grew fearful by the day about their safety and future in America. My family was no exception. We began to fear the people who had welcomed us into America. There were countless stories of Muslims being harassed and attacked for their appearance. Some had even been killed. Hate crimes against the Muslim community in America soared. Some mosques and the Qur'an, Islam's holy book, were burned. Out of fear, some American Muslim women stopped wearing their headscarves. Likewise, some Muslim men no longer put the *kufi* hat on their heads. Some even went so far as not attending prayers in their local mosques. A few even changed their names to Anglo-American names. I never thought that my name or my faith were the issue.

After all, Thomas Jefferson would have burned the Qur'an after reading it if there were an issue with the Islamic holy book. "Islam has been a piece of the American religious fabric since the first settlers arrived in North America. . . . African Muslims were an integral part of creating America from mapping its borders to fighting against British rule. Muslims first came to North America in the 1500s as part of colonial expeditions."[10] Many of the enslaved African Americans were Muslims. "The founding fathers were aware of Islam and the presence of Muslims in America. Thomas Jefferson, who owned a copy of the Qur'an, included Islam in many of his

10   Ayla Amon, "American Muslims in Early America," National Museum of African American History & Culture, https://nmaahc.si.edu/explore/stories/collection/african-muslims-early-america.

early writings and political treatises. Campaigning for religious freedom in Virginia, Jefferson argued in the proposed 'Virginia Statute for Religious Freedom' that, 'neither Pagan, nor Mahamedan [Muslim], nor Jew ought to be excluded from the civil rights of the Commonwealth because of his religion.'"[11] The Virginia Statute for Religious Freedom became a law on January 16, 1786. "It is the forerunner of the first amendment protections for religious freedom."[12] In a nutshell, Islam played a role in crafting our First Amendment, the freedom of religion in the Constitution. However, more than 226 years after the First Amendment was adopted in December 1791, Islam and Muslims are still seen as foreign as ever to many Americans.

The bright side is that even in the midst of such a tragedy as 9/11, there was enormous goodwill by the majority of Americans. Soon after the 9/11 attacks, I remember interfaith community leaders from multiple denominations coming to our Islamic Association of Raleigh Mosque on a Saturday afternoon. They reassured us that they stood with us and that there was nothing to fear.

Still, the Muslim community experienced fear. We didn't know who to trust. We feared being associated with someone who may be under investigation. There was a cold period right after the 9/11 attacks. Some people weren't comfortable giving their phone numbers to people they'd met at the mosque for fear of association. My family was lucky not to be harassed or attacked. But, several years after the attacks, the wife of one of my best friends was verbally assaulted at a gas station in Irving, Texas. Another friend was interrogated at Dulles airport for hours because of his name and his travel to Saudi Arabia. The negative effects of 9/11 on Muslims in America still exist.

To me, there's irony when it comes to Americans decrying immigration. Those same Americans' predecessors likely immigrated to America

11   Amon, "American Muslims in Early America".
12   Virginia Museum of History & Culture, "Thomas Jefferson and the Virginia Statute for Religious Freedom," https://www.virginiahistory.org/collections-and-resources/virginia-history-explorer/thomas-jefferson

for the same reasons new immigrants still arrive: security, freedom, and opportunity. America is a collection of yesterday and today's immigrants. America remains a favored destination for most immigrants whether they're fleeing persecution or poverty, and I believe that says much about America's image to the world. However, America should worry about its future when immigrants no longer want to migrate here.

In January 2002, a severe snowstorm was scheduled to hit Raleigh. Since we didn't have a snow shovel, I asked my brother-in-law, Luul's husband, to ride with me to Home Depot. Despite his protestations that he didn't want to go out so soon before the storm was scheduled to start, we got into my Geo Metro and drove just four miles to Home Depot. The snow fell slowly upon us, likely heightening my brother-in-law's anxiety. He *had* lived in Canada for many years, so maybe he had the right to be nervous.

But I was a naive twenty-three-year-old. We could make it. We rushed into the store, bought the snow shovel, then rushed back into our car. The snow was falling harder and blanketing the road. *We can make it*, I thought. *It's just four miles.*

Unfortunately, those four miles included a snow-driven curve that I took at too high a speed. I even remember my brother-in-law telling me to slow down before we hit that curve on Buck Jones Road. My small Metro slid to the right of the curve and plowed into another car. The cars behind me piled up on the driver's side, pinning my door shut. As soon as our car finally came to a stop—the crash felt like it had taken an eternity—I realized there was a downslope lurking just behind the oak trees behind us. I feared we would slide off even further at any second.

The passenger-side door was also blocked by other cars, so my brother-in-law couldn't exit. He tried to pull me to the passenger side, but he couldn't budge me. He climbed out of his window and tried to get to me from outside of the car. Others came to help. One person asked, "Can you stand up a little bit?" Of course, that person didn't know about me. I said,

"I can't." With others helping my brother-in-law, he pulled me through the driver's side window, and then they pulled my wheelchair through. They placed me in my wheelchair, where I could see my legs had been bruised by the ordeal. I was also freezing. Seeing my sad state, my brother-in-law wheeled me to a nearby gas station so we could warm up. As luck would have it, I knew the gas station's owner. He offered us a ride home in his four-wheel SUV—a car much more suited for a snowstorm than a Geo Metro, driven by a driver who wasn't so arrogant as to believe he could just force his way through any difficulty.

11 Stretching Beyond My Limits

In the weeks following the accident, I felt muscle pain in my back, which was nothing necessarily new. To complicate matters, I'd had a sore on the small toe of my left foot. These were the kinds of medical issues I dealt with on a daily basis. Of course, it was uncomfortable—at least the pain sensations that I could feel. Remember: I have no sensation from my waist down. So, I could see the sore on my toe, but I couldn't feel it. Unfortunately, that's something you'll need to remember for this next part.

I applied ointment to that sore on my toe every morning. On January 23, 2002, I lifted my left foot onto my right thigh to inspect my toe. Because I couldn't feel if it was healed, I could only look to see about its progress. On that day, I pulled my foot closer and closer to my face—then a spasm erupted. Not thinking anything of it, because spasms were a regular part of my day, I kept pulling my leg closer until I heard a pop.

My stomach cringed.

I touched my left femur and quickly realized I'd broken it.

At the time, my father was there. I yelled, "Dad! Dad!"

He rushed into the bathroom. "What's going on, Abdi?"

"I broke my left femur!"

"What do you mean? How could you break your femur?" Before I could answer, he touched my left leg, and the blood drained from his face.

I called 911 and reported that I'd broken my left femur. The operator couldn't understand what I was saying, and the more I tried to explain, the more confused she seemed to become. However, she dispatched an ambulance to us. A few minutes later, I was stabilized on a stretcher and being rushed to Rex Hospital, our nearest ER. On the short ride there, my mind vacillated between shock—I never thought in a million years I could break my own leg—and acceptance: I'd been paralyzed since 1991, for the last eleven years. Of course the bones in my legs would be fragile.

Once I'd been assessed in the ER, they scheduled me for surgery later that day. The young doctor who'd perform the surgery—he seemed like he had just turned thirty—walked into the room, looked at my leg, then asked, "Do you feel it?"

Annoyed, I replied, "No."

"Then why do you want it fixed? Why don't we cut it out so you won't have to go through the long healing process?"

I couldn't believe what I was hearing, but I didn't let on how shocked I was by his questions. "I need it fixed, Doc."

He just nodded. I still wonder why he would have said such a thing.

That afternoon, the baby-faced doctor placed a long metal rod from near my hip joint to my knee. I recuperated at the hospital for a couple of days, and then I was transferred to WakeMed in Raleigh because they had a better rehabilitation facility. I rehabbed at WakeMed for a couple of weeks. I fell down in the shower a few times and had to call for the nurses' help. But that rehab wasn't as bad as what I'd endured before.

While at Rex, I'd called Wake Tech Community College to inform them about my accident. I requested that they drop me from all of my current courses so that I wouldn't fail. Gratefully, they understood and were willing to help me in this time of need.

When my family and friends heard about the injury, they were shocked and saddened. Their grief affected me, but not in the way most would have suspected. I'd endured so much more than just this broken bone. I became even more determined to get past this momentary setback. After long sessions of rehab both at the hospital and at home, I regained my independence.

And I made a mental note never to stretch my legs that way again.

———————

I became a full citizen of the United States in April of 2002, ready and willing to make positive contributions to my adopted and beloved country. Even though anti-Muslim sentiment was high at that time in the wake of 9/11, at least as far as the media was reporting, I knew that most Americans weren't that way because of the many men and women I'd met since I'd come to America. I also knew that this land of opportunity had provided me with just that: opportunity after opportunity after opportunity. When I'd reflect on my life before and after coming to America, I could only be thankful for the sacrifices my family, and particularly my father, had made in bringing me across the Atlantic.

That's one reason why saying good-bye to my father in May of 2002 was so difficult. That's when he'd decided to move back to Somalia for good. I didn't blame him. When he asked me what I thought about him moving away, I told him it was OK. He'd given up so much so that I could have a higher quality of life than I could have expected. Who was I to ask any more of him? He'd stuck by my side until I was finally able to live alone. Plus, he was seventy-two at the time, didn't speak English, and had had a difficult time adjusting to life in the United States. He didn't work and wound up staying at home most of the time while he lived with me. So when he asked to go, I understood. It was time for me to explore the world on my own—however difficult that would be without his constant presence near me.

Still, our parting was bittersweet. I knew it would be unlikely for me to ever see him again for a number of reasons. He was old and only getting older. Mogadishu was still just as unsafe as it had been when we'd left. And if I were ever able to travel back to Somalia, they likely wouldn't have the accommodations I'd need to get there and stay there for any length of time. Upon his departure, our long-held hug felt like the last time I'd ever feel his love envelop me again.

A few days after his arrival in Mogadishu, I called to inquire about his travel, which he said had gone just fine. Every few weeks, I'd call him and my mother to check on them. And when I heard terrible news from Mogadishu, an all-too-common occurrence in the early 2000s, I'd call them again. Suicide bombings were sadly a normal part of life in Somalia. I feared for my parents' safety any time I thought of them.

No longer was I the child about whom they were anxious and afraid. Now I was the fearful parent, always calling to ensure their safety. Now it seemed like I truly was an adult.

———————

Then again, my parents had a right to worry.

On a frigid day in February of 2003, I was headed to an appointment to upgrade my wheelchair. I cranked the heat up to warm my shivering body. Without warning, smoke began seeping through the A/C vent!

Let's pause here and recount my last vehicular episode, the one where I thought I could take a snow-banked curve at a high rate of speed.

I hadn't learned my lesson. Except this time, I didn't speed up. I just kept going.

As more smoke billowed out, I slowed down. Eventually, I knew something was wrong. Just as I pulled to the curb and opened my door, *fire* had taken the place of the smoke. My wheelchair was still in the backseat. *How in the world am I going to get out of this? I can't run away without reassembling my wheelchair!*

My next thought—which was not my best thought—was, *Maybe I can put the fire out with a seat cushion. That should buy me some time.*

All it bought me was *more fire.* The flames ate the cushion.

Not knowing what else to do, I frantically put my wheelchair together, silently praying to Allah to save me from the growing flames.

Less than a minute later, I'd placed my wheelchair on the ground beside me and, with the help of bystanders who didn't want to get too close, I managed to slide over without being grazed by the flames. I don't know how that had been possible because, as I looked back into the car, the dashboard was engulfed. My prayers had been answered.

A few minutes after a State Trooper had arrived, my Geo Metro's windows shattered from the heat. The fire, unsated by my offering of a seat cushion, was now devouring my favorite and only mode of high-speed transportation. I watched in shock and awe. That car had been my equalizer; it gave me the freedom to do everything I loved to do. *What would I do now?* Even as I thought that, I knew I should be beyond grateful for not having suffered bodily harm. The outcome of that disastrous ride could have been much worse.

The trooper corroborated my thinking. "You're lucky to have gotten out. You can always recover material things."

I nodded my head in full agreement. The trooper then offered me a ride home, which I gratefully accepted.

On our way there, he asked, "Where are you from?"

"Somalia."

"Mogadishu?"

With surprise, I said yes, then asked, "How do you know Mogadishu?"

"I was deployed there in 1993 on a mission to arrest General Mohamed Farah Aidiid."

I couldn't believe what I was hearing. He'd been in my country when I'd been in my country! We each then shared our respective stories about how we'd come to be in Raleigh, North Carolina. Maybe I met that trooper on that day as a result of my prayers. Maybe I needed to be reminded of how far I'd come.

I don't know what caused the fire. I'd been doing routine oil changes. But that car consumed a lot of oil. Maybe I had insufficient oil, or maybe it was a fuse problem.

A few days after the accident, my brother Mustafa and I searched for a new (used) car. We found another Geo Metro with low mileage and sold as-is for eighteen hundred dollars. I only had sixteen hundred dollars to put toward the car, so my sister Luul came through yet again, knowing how essential having a car was to me. She gave me a thousand dollars to cover the full cost of the car plus the hand-control installment. I bought the car with cash the next day. A few days later, I had the hand control equipment installed for another eight hundred dollars. Within two weeks of the fiery accident, I was ready to get back to being productive.

I told my parents what happened. My father replied with what he'd always say to me: "Son, my prayers are with you. May Allah always protect you and guide you."

———————

A little less than a year earlier, in June 2002, I'd returned to Wake Tech for two summer courses. The instructors who knew me from the student learning center asked where I'd been. I told them my story, and I could tell by the looks on their faces how empathetic they were. They verbally expressed their sorrow over what had happened to me. But what's funny to me today is that I never felt sorry for myself—not then, and still not today. I always rolled forward. I never concentrated on my setbacks, knowing that that would never get me to where I wanted to be. I always looked ahead to what tomorrow could bring. Whenever I took stock of my life—even despite its hardships—I was grateful for what I had.

In fact, on more than one occasion, I became someone else's comforter. After relating some part of my story, whether my most recent accident or the bombing that had forever changed my life, some people became emotional. They didn't see how I could have withstood so much, and especially at a young age. So I'd do my best to comfort them, letting them know that life can be hard, but it doesn't have to be impossible. I also never lost my sense of humor—which definitely helped in situations like those. As far as I know, my father never pitied me. I didn't want anyone else to either. So putting on a brave face, even when the physical pain was close to unbearable, was a common occurrence during my day.

After completing those summer courses and a full course load that ensuing fall, I opted to transfer to North Carolina State University, which was also in Raleigh. I received my acceptance letter into NCSU's College of Management in the spring of 2003. I was inwardly proud of the hard work and determination I'd put into ensuring my success in my studies. Even though the broken-leg incident had set my timeline back, it hadn't fully prevented me from my ultimate goal: a college degree.

Of course, it wasn't clear sailing. I heavily relied on my sister during these years, and I fondly remember the breakfast meals she'd make for me every morning before I drove to the campus, which was just a few minutes from our home. But in the fall of 2004, she endured a divorce. Consequently, she moved back to Somalia, taking her two-year-old son, Bilal, with her. I missed them immensely. Her absence also meant another challenge of independence I'd have to overcome: cooking for myself on a regular basis. While focusing on my studies to get my degree, I taught myself how to cook and how to be a good grocery shopper. (Never once did I mistakenly buy dog food—as far as I know.)

Maybe it was the loss of those few months with my broken leg that truly motived me during my last two years of college. I graduated from NCSU several months ahead of schedule in May of 2005 with a bachelor of science in supply chain management. My brother Mustafa and my friend, Bootaan, attended my graduation ceremony at the Wolfpack's basketball arena, the RBC Center, on May 14, 2005. They hollered for me as loudly as they could as I rolled across the stage, grabbed my diploma, and raised my hands over my head in celebration. Mustafa took pictures.

I vividly remember talking to my classmates, some of whom were going to graduate schools, while others were seeking jobs in corporate America. Anne Lyford, who was NCSU's College of Management career counselor and had helped prepare me for my job search, was also there cheering for our class. There was a lot of excitement, congratulatory notes, and well-wishes. It was a joyous day.

Less than ten years after the happiest day of my life, when my father and I had landed at Dulles for the first time, I experienced the second happiest day of my life. But it was bittersweet. The man who'd pushed me in so many ways to achieve this monumental goal wasn't there to see it happen.

But he certainly heard all about it later.

12 Singular Accomplishments

Upon my graduation, I had to land a job as soon as possible. Although I'd entertained going to grad school, financial circumstances surrounding my family dictated that I needed to find a job. I couldn't "waste" two more years in school. I needed to start earning money so that I could financially support my family back in Somalia.

One chief reason I needed to help was that my sister Ureeji had suffered a miscarriage. She'd been ill during her pregnancy, and the child had died within her womb during the last weeks of the pregnancy. She developed high blood pressure and other medical complications. The surgery to remove her lost child was devastating. And, of course, her medical needs cost money that my parents didn't have. For as much as my sister and my parents had provided for me over the years, it was my duty to now help them.

So, even a few months before my graduation, I worked closely with the career placement office at NCSU to find suitable job prospects for a supply chain management major. The first relevant option appeared 133 miles away, at a Walmart distribution center near Richmond, Virginia. I'd met a Walmart recruiter at a job fair in the spring of 2005, and he'd recommended that I visit their facility and interview with their hiring manager.

I was thrilled at the prospect. A distribution center is exactly where a man with a degree in supply chain management should work. I thought, *I'll have a job in no time.*

When the day of my visit arrived, I dressed in a black suit and tie. I also invited my cousin, Abdul Aziz, to take the two-and-a-half-hour trip with me. He obliged, but he also dampened my expectations during our drive. He questioned whether I'd really commute so long to such a remote area. Too excited about landing a job so quickly, I hadn't thought too much about the distance. I had to admit to myself: even though I loved my car, it would be difficult to give five hours of my day just to driving. But we were already on the way, and I knew I would sacrifice what I had to in order to land any professional job.

When the hiring manager greeted us, he seemed surprised to see me. I imagine he was wondering why a man in a wheelchair was interviewing for a position at a distribution center, where access was less than ideal. He led us on a tour of the entire facility before my interview. Then he inquired about my education and work experience. I handed him my rather scant resume. It showed no work history—because I had none. As the interview ended, he said they'd be in touch. A few days later, I received a disheartening email from their human resources department. Another candidate had been selected.

I was dejected for a moment, but I used that rejection to fuel my further search. However, had I known I would look for a job for the next six months, I probably wouldn't have been so optimistic. More than a few times, I wondered if my disability was preventing me from obtaining jobs I knew I could do. Then again, I also realized I was a recent college graduate without experience and the kinds of jobs I was seeking had competition.

———————

While at the NCSU career development office in October 2005, I overheard that Cingular Wireless (now AT&T) had created the College Hire (now B2B Sales) program and would be conducting interviews on campus *tomorrow*. An adviser in the office, who knew how hard I'd been searching for a job, told me that a few interview spots were still open. Was I interested? Of course I was.

The next day, dressed in my black suit and tie, I handed Charlotte and Courtney my still-scant resume. They inquired about my educational background and work experience. I related how much I'd learned over the years and conveyed how driven I was to succeed at everything I attempted. Then they asked me a few situational questions, one of which made me smile inside.

"Have you ever dealt with any challenging issues? If so, how did you resolve them?"

Oh, the stories I could have told them.

"I've overcome many challenges in my life. Far too many to tell you all about right now. But I'll share this story. Back in 2002, my sister's husband had to travel back to Somalia, effectively leaving me to watch over her. This wouldn't have been too big of a deal, but my sister, Luul, was seven months pregnant. On July 30th, I took her to her pediatric doctor for a checkup. He discovered that her blood pressure was too high and asserted that a C-section would have to be performed that night for the safety of both the mother and the baby."

The interviewers were rapt with attention.

"So I immediately took my sister to the hospital that night, where they performed the C-section. Mother and child were just fine, even though little Bilal weighed only four pounds at birth. However, because the little guy had arrived so early, my sister and brother-in-law had yet to prepare their house for their new arrival. So, as my sister and new nephew recuperated at the hospital for those next few days, I went shopping for baby clothes and a crib. I made sure to get everything I knew to get for a new baby."

The women smiled.

"When I brought her and Bilal home, my sister was so surprised to see a clean house, new baby clothes, and a crib. Over the next few days, I took her to her doctor's appointments and bought baby formula. I was a stand-in, er, sit-down father for her new baby. A few weeks after his birth, my sister's husband returned from Somalia. I was grateful to have been helpful, but I was also relieved to be relieved of my duties."

They thanked me for sharing such a personal story. As we wrapped up the interview, they said if I were selected as a possible candidate for a position within the company, I'd have to do a second interview. I nodded, thanked them for their time, and rolled out. I thought the interview had gone well. I'd answered every question with honesty and passion, and I thought sharing such a personal story was a good touch. But I'd been through so many interviews by that point that I wasn't sure of myself anymore. Even if it had gone as well as it could, I didn't know who else they'd been interviewing or how many open positions they had for recent college grads.

I wheeled away optimistic but realistic.

A few days later, my ringing phone roused me from a nap. Not quite awake, I said, "Hello? Who's this?"

"This is Cingular Wireless's human resources. Is this Mr. Warsame?"

I snapped awake, fully alert. "Yes, yes! This is Abdi Warsame."

"Do you have a few minutes to talk, Mr. Warsame?"

"Of course."

"Are you willing to relocate to—"

"Yes." Before she'd even finished her sentence, I'd said yes.

At the moment I'd agreed, she completed her question: "to Atlanta?" She laughed at my quick answer, then proceeded to tell me further details about the job Cingular Wireless was offering me. "You'll have to go through a rigorous six-month training program in Atlanta. If you complete that training successfully, you'll be placed in one of our markets as a sale rep selling our products and services. But you have to be in Atlanta before January 10th. That's when our College Hire training begins." We discussed further details, then, before our conversation ended, she asked, "Do you accept our—"

I cut her off again. "Yes. Yes! I accept your offer."

"Be sure to send me your confirmation via email too."

"Of course. Thank you so much for this opportunity."

"Thanks for your time, Mr. Warsame. All the best at your training. Cingular Wireless welcomes you. Good-bye."

I said good-bye and hung up. I should have taken a photo of my beaming face at that moment. I couldn't wait to tell my parents, my extended family, and my friends that I had finally landed a job. I was proud to show them the kind of person I'd become due to their many sacrifices on my behalf. Now I'd be able to truly help them.

The first person I relayed my good news to was my brother Mustafa.

"I've accepted a position with Cingular Wireless!"

"Congratulations, Abdi. Where's it located?"

"Atlanta."

"Atlanta, *Georgia*?"

"Yes, exactly."

"How is that possible? Are you telling me that you're, in effect, thinking to uproot yourself and leave everything behind to venture out to a place more than four hundred miles away for a job that's *not* one hundred percent guaranteed?"

"Yes," I replied cautiously.

"You're crazy."

I was rather shocked by his reaction. Didn't he know I could take care of myself by then? But, in looking back, maybe I'm being too presumptive. Maybe he was just trying to look out for me, like he always had. My cousins in Raleigh agreed with my brother. They all thought my move would be a bad idea. They urged me to stay in Raleigh and seek a job closer to home. They feared that my wheelchair would cause all kinds of problems with the move, at a new job, and in a new town. But didn't they know how small those issues seemed to me? Hadn't they seen how much I'd already overcome?

Back then (and even today), I never thought of my physical limitations as a barrier against pursuing any opportunity. I always believed that I should never sell myself short. Despite my family's misgivings about my move, I had no second thoughts. This was the right move for me.

In hindsight, it was one of the best decisions I've ever made.

Although Cingular didn't offer relocation assistance to cover the costs of my move, they did provide something better: full apartment accommodations in the upscale Dunwoody neighborhood, which was less than a mile away from the B2B Sales program center where I would train for the next six months. To offset my moving costs and make the trip easier on myself, I auctioned or gave away most of my belongings.

During that transitional time, I discovered that I had relatives in Atlanta. (I told you: I have relatives everywhere!) I'd known my cousin Amina since living in Mombasa, and I was gladly surprised to learn she was now living in Atlanta. She assured me that she'd help make my new home just like my old home. Although I knew I was heading to Atlanta no matter the circumstances, knowing that a family member lived there assuaged my fears about moving to a new place all by myself.

Additionally, I'd recently met Omar, a Sudanese friend, at the Islamic Center of Raleigh. In our conversations, we both learned that we'd soon be traveling to Atlanta—me for my new job and Omar to pick up a car. He suggested that we ride together, and I was more than happy to agree.

On Saturday, January 7, 2006, my brother Mustafa drove me to the rental car location at Raleigh Durham International Airport. We arrived at 6 a.m. Within the hour, I gave Mustafa a parting hug and thanked him for everything he'd done for me since my arrival in America. Without his help, I would never have had the opportunity for a trip—or a job—like this. Yet again, I realized how essential my family was to my ongoing journey toward success.

Per my request, a hand-control device had been installed in the rental car. I drove to Omar's house in east Raleigh. From there, I drove halfway to Atlanta. Since Omar had been to Atlanta before and knew the streets, he drove the second leg. No adverse weather affected our drive. It was a beautiful morning in so many ways.

As we left Raleigh, I peered outside of the window and to the side of the highway while driving, reminiscing about what that city had meant to me. I'd moved there nine years earlier, barely able to speak English. My outlook on my future was less than uncertain. Once I was told there'd be no surgery or medicine that could heal my spinal cord injury, I knew my only path toward success was education. In Raleigh, I had rolled from Athens High School, to Wake Tech, and finally to NCSU. Now I was driving myself to my first job to live wholly independently for the first time in my life. I was an educated, confident man with a brighter, more hopeful future. I thanked God for the opportunities I'd been given and the open roads that now lay before me.

A few minutes after our arrival at my new apartment in Atlanta, my cousin Amina called. "Are you here?"

I could hear the excitement in her voice. I answered yes, and she said she'd be right over.

I surveyed my new apartment and was surprised by how luxurious it was. I thought, *This is really happening. Finally, I'm about to test the fruits of all my hard work after years of pursuing a higher education.*

An hour later, my cousin and an aunt arrived, and they were kind enough to have brought a big Somali-style lunch: rice, spaghetti, goat meat, salad, and homemade fruit juice. I devoured it, but I also said, "You've brought too much!"

They laughed and replied, "Keep the leftovers in your fridge. You'll need it."

Omar dined with us, and his ride picked him up soon after we'd all finished eating. Before his departure, he asked me, "You're coming back to Raleigh, right?"

"Of course. I'll see you in Raleigh in six months." When I'd taken the limited-term Atlanta assignment, it was my hope that they'd place me back in Raleigh once my training was over.

The rest of that day was filled with laughter and reminiscing with family members whom I hadn't seen in years. When they asked about my new job, I told them all about it. They were happy to hear that my workplace was just down the street. I joked that I could walk there if necessary.

Little did I know that I'd be eating my words just a few days later!

I began working for Cingular Wireless on Tuesday, January 10, 2006. At a meet-and-greet the day before, the twenty-two new hires were warned by the staffing manager, "You are expected to be on the sixteenth floor of the Abernathy building no later than 8 a.m. tomorrow in a suit and tie."

I had my one suit and tie, but I still didn't have my car. It would still be a few days before it was transported from Raleigh to Atlanta. So I had to figure out some way to get to work for at least a week—and I didn't want to ask favors of people I didn't know.

On the first full day of my new job, I awoke at 5:30 a.m. I showered, got dressed in my suit and tie, prayed, and ate breakfast. Then I called a taxi and was dropped off at the Abernathy building well before 8 a.m. I repeated the process the next morning, but the taxi service said they'd be late. I couldn't risk waiting, so I followed the only route that was left to me: I wheeled myself a mile down the road. I might have been a little sweaty, but I arrived before 8 a.m. After having come so far—much farther than that mile-long path would show—I wasn't going to give up so easily or allow my disability to disbar me from succeeding at my new job.

Later that day, I was chatting with Eric Bishop, another new hire like me. He casually inquired how I'd gotten to work that day. I told him I'd wheeled there. He was surprised by my dedication to the job, then he surprised me by offering me a ride home. Turns out—and I should have thought about this before trying to do so much on my own—he lived at the same apartment complex, as did most of the recent hires (of course). For the next few days, until my car arrived, Eric gave me a ride to and from work. I hadn't expected that kind of generosity from a stranger, but I was grateful for his help. I would eventually learn that his father also used a wheelchair. Consequently, Eric had a deeper understanding of people with disabilities who'd dealt with some of life's ultimate challenges.

I received my first paycheck after two weeks. Since my only suit and tie had become a noticeable fixture at my job—where I felt surrounded by well-groomed graduates from middle- to upper-class families—I immediately upgraded my wardrobe and bought more suits and ties.

Now with attire befitting a Corporate Sales Executive, I was given a monthly quota to hit by cold-calling existing small business customers and persuading them to upgrade their contracts and devices from the aging TDMA network to Cingular's newer GSM network. They were incentivized to upgrade to a two-year contract with the lure of free mobile devices. If we didn't hit our quotas, we ran the risk of being let go from the program.

Thanks to the help and training I'd received from Rick, an experienced call center rep, I hit my first quota of seventeen migrated lines in February 2006. The next month, I struck a gold mine. By migrating the Monterey Bay Aquarium in California and selling them new lines of service, I'd tripled my quota. My commission on those sales was the largest check I'd ever received. For the month of March, I was the undisputed king of the call center.

The following month, our placement process began. When asked to rank the top three markets in which I wanted to be placed, I named Central North Carolina (Raleigh), Atlanta, and South Carolina. While my colleagues were interviewing with sales managers in their respective top choices, I wasn't offered anything. I became disappointed and wondered where I'd be going. Still, I focused on my training and met or exceeded my quotas for the remaining months of the program.

Turns out, I'd done *too* well. In June 2006, the training program's director asked if I'd like to stay in Atlanta with the training program and support their Virtual Sales Channel (VSC). I gladly accepted the position of Sales Execution Program Analyst. By the end of 2007, I'd help migrate approximately three million customers to the GSM network. During my three-year tenure as analyst, I supported the VSC in crafting a new fraud-containment process, by launching multiple promotional campaigns, and in developing their strategic plan, budget, and sales forecast.

All from the perch of my well-traveled wheelchair.

13 The More Things Change

Even though it had been more than a decade since I'd left Africa, Somalia was never far from my mind. Because my mother, father, siblings, and so many of my relatives still lived there, I closely monitored events in the Horn of Africa. No news was always good news. Unfortunately, when there was news from Somalia, it was bad news nine times out of ten.

Some historical information is helpful here, but it may sound redundant from the earliest chapters of my book. In Somalia, not much had changed. The names of the people and organizations may have been different, but the underlying motivations for power and control remained the same. In the mid-2000s, Mogadishu was still divided. However, instead of one or two major players vying for control, the country feared a number of ruthless warlords, all of whom were vying for power. Residents hated them but felt helpless to stop them.

Fortunately, Islamic courts had sprung up in the wake of the vacuum of power that had been created after the end of the civil war. These courts provided rulings on issues ranging from property disputes, damages claims, homicides, and more. The courts filled the gap where the country had yet to implement a central government or judicial system. Because the courts meted out justice without the use of arms, their popularity rose dramatically—and so much so that the warlords took notice and created their own ironically named group: the Alliance for the Restoration of Peace and Counter-Terrorism (ARPCT). Author Eben Kaplan aptly described ARPCT's motives: "Despite its name, the ARPCT probably does little to combat terrorism and is more interested in maintaining the lawless status quo in which the warlords thrive."[13] Under pressure, the unaffiliated Islamic courts formed their own alliance: the Union of Islamic Courts (UIC). They chose a young and charismatic man, Sharif Sheikh Ahmed, as their leader. (In 2009, he would become Somalia's president.)

On February 18, 2006, the UIC clashed with the ARPCT. Fighting, as it had a habit of doing, erupted in the streets of Mogadishu yet again. On June 5, the UIC prevailed and regained control of Mogadishu. For the first time since January 1991—the month and year I'd suffered my life-changing injury—the UIC had established a single administrative rule over Mogadishu. Emboldened by their success against the ARPCT, the UIC expanded its control to further territories in central and south Somalia. Mogadishu residents enjoyed peace for the first time in decades, ever since Barre had been ousted—but peace would last for only six months.

Based in Baidoa, a city northwest of Mogadishu, the Transitional Federal Government (TFG) was another governmental entity put in place to help bring order to chaos. That entity had been created in October 2004 following a reconciliation conference in Kenya and had moved into Somalia in February 2006. During a conference on June 22, 2006, in Khartoum, Sudan, the TFG and the UIC attempted to work out their differences for a peaceful coexistence. They agreed to stop military hostilities between each other and to continue negotiations. But, at the follow-up talks on September 1, 2006, the TFG and the UIC couldn't reach a solution.

Fearing that the UIC would capture Baidoa, the TFG requested Ethiopia to protect them. For its part, Ethiopia had long been involved in Somali affairs, including supporting the former warlords and even pitting them against each other. In July 2006, Ethiopia dispatched an estimated ten thousand troops to Baidoa. Five months later, the UIC declared war

---

13   Eben Kaplan, "Somalia's High Stakes Power Struggle," Council on Foreign
       Relations, https://www.cfr.org/backgrounder/somalias-high-stakes-power-struggle.

on the TFG. Conflict finally erupted on December 20, 2006, near Baidoa. After several days of sustained battles, the Ethiopian-backed TFG overcame UIC's forces. By the end of December, the UIC has also lost control of much of the territories it had once governed—including Mogadishu.

Possibly even more concerning was that that UIC's defeat led to a military wing forming out of the UIC. Known as the Al-Shabaab terrorist group, they would go on to perpetrate some of the most heinous bombings in Somalia.

The TFG moved into Mogadishu in early 2007 and immediately imposed its authority. An insurgency was mounted throughout the South by remnants of the Islamic courts accompanied by clan militias who felt occupied by the Ethiopian forces. In response, the TFG ordered that certain neighborhoods north of Mogadishu evacuate their homes or face bombardment.

My family lived in one of those neighborhoods.

Once again, warring factions in Somalia were forcefully moving my family, and none of us had any control over it.

Now you know why I closely monitored the news.

Some 335,000 Somalis were displaced in the 2007 Mogadishu conflict.[14] Many moved somewhere else in Somalia, but others—with the financial means to do so—moved to neighboring countries like Kenya, Ethiopia, and Djibouti. Moving to one of those countries was a better option than just moving across Somalia, but it was also costlier. However, because of my position with AT&T, I could afford to help.

Concerned about my parents' safety, I offered both my mother and father an option to get out of the country if they wanted to move to a neighboring country. My mother was more than ready to leave Somalia.

---

14 "Routinely targeted Attacks on civilians in Somalia," amnesty international, last modified May 6, 2008, https://www.amnesty.org/download/Documents/52000/afr520092008eng.pdf.

I contacted my younger brother, Farhan, who then lived in Addis Ababa, Ethiopia, and asked him to rent a place for our family. I sent my mother some money and booked flights for her and for my older sisters, Halima and Ureeji, and for Ureeji's four children.

My father, who was then living with his second wife and had two young sons and one daughter, opted to remain in Somalia. However, they would be moving to Barawe, a historical town on the Indian Ocean a little over one hundred miles south of Mogadishu.

Part of me wonders if my father's decision to stay in Somalia was motivated by his concern for my financial well-being. Knowing that I had to take care of myself, my sister, Luul—a story I'll share in the next chapter—and my mother's moving expenses, he might have chosen the smaller move to help me save money. He was just that way.

Even though it wasn't easy to get my family out of Mogadishu, I was grateful for my abilities to do so. Looking back, I'm proud that I helped them escape Mogadishu's misery. I know my parents were proud too. They thanked me for working so hard and providing them with a steady, monthly stream of funding. I just know that if something like what happened to me would have happened to them, I would have never forgiven myself.

During that time, I received many more calls for assistance, financial and otherwise, from more immediate family members trapped in Mogadishu. I'm not a person to turn away from people who need help, so I helped as much as I could, even given my limited resources. I had been given so much by so many people during my life that it felt selfish to do any less.

Prior to the mass displacement occurring in Mogadishu in 2007 that forced my parents out, my sister Luul and her son, Bilal, had returned to the United States from Somalia in May. They would stay with me for the next five years. During that time, my sister fought incredible hardships, which I'll speak to in the following chapter. I mention it here because, while she and I struggled with her mental health issues, our sister Ureeji fought her own health battles in Addis Ababa.

From what I understand, Ureeji's health problems stemmed from having high blood pressure. Giving birth to her youngest son, Zachariah, only exacerbated her high blood pressure. She soon suffered a stroke, which negatively affected her right arm and leg. She received treatment and therapy, but she suffered another stroke two months later. This stroke, unfortunately, was massive. In September 2009, she was taken to a hospital in Addis Ababa and slipped into a coma.

A few days later, she died.

When I received the news of my dear sister's passing, it was in the last ten days of the holy month of Ramadan. I'd been fasting, so it felt like the news of her death struck me even more deeply. The following days were brutal. The more I thought about Ureeji, the harder it became to acknowledge that she was forever gone.

I called my mother in a vain attempt at consolation. Until death had parted them, they had been inseparable. The only time I know of that they'd even been apart was when my mother went to the Hajj, the annual Muslim pilgrimage to Mecca, Saudi Arabia, or when Ureeji went to Dubai for treatment. Apart from those times, Ureeji had been at our mother's side since birth.

I thought it a little strange that I should be calling to comfort my mother. She's the most resilient person I know. She'd lost her beautiful child (and my sister), Rahma, in a car accident when Rahma was three. According to what I've been told, when they brought Rahma's body into the house, my mother didn't scream or curse. She quietly mourned the loss of her baby child. She understood that Rahma—which means mercy—wasn't meant to grow up in this world, and that we weren't meant to cherish her into adulthood.

Now I knew what it felt like to lose a sister. I hated it.

Ureeji had been a pillar in our family—our most tenacious, most compassionate member. She'd gotten us through very difficult times in the 1990s, when it seemed as if chaos were our homeland. She was an incredibly smart businesswoman. With her earnings, she'd even bought the houses our mother and father had lived in in Mogadishu. She was the one who had supported my father and me seeking treatment in Kenya.

She was very near to my heart for all those reasons and more. I loved her immensely, and I still miss her every day.

———

After Ureeji's passing, my mother hated Addis Ababa. It had become a place of hollow ground, a constant reminder of the daughter she'd lost. Without Ureeji, my mother felt lost and alone. She was also barely getting by at this time. So I shouldn't have been surprised when I received a phone call from my mother informing me that she was moving back to Mogadishu.

I tried to reason with her. "Mother, it's not safe enough in Mogadishu for you to return. Please reconsider."

"Abdi, I have already decided to go back. You cannot change my mind." I knew that to be the truth.

She continued. "I need to safeguard our family properties anyways."

I think that's the reasoning she told herself to make her move back to Mogadishu a rational decision. I still didn't want her to go, fearful of the fighting that was still going on in Somalia. But I also understood why she would want to leave Addis Ababa. I made no argument against her, and I sent money to assist with plane tickets.

A few days later, accompanied by her brother, Abdullahi, they arrived in Mogadishu. However, they couldn't go straight to her house. There was too much fighting. Government forces, assisted by African Union forces, were warring against the Al Shabaab fighters. My mother rented a place in a neighborhood near the city center.

To hear about how they were trapped even upon their immediate arrival was difficult and nerve-racking.

Then what I had long feared would happen happened, though not to my mother.

Before my mother had finally been able to move back into her house, an eighteen-year-old distant nephew of mine, Mohamed, was struck by a bullet as he was entering her home. He had been living at my mother's house at the time. Young Zachariah saw him fall and raced to tell my mother about what had just occurred. My mother sprinted to the front door and called for help. Mohamed was then quickly taken to the nearest hospital, where the doctors discovered that his injury was not life-threatening. He'd been hit in the leg, and it hadn't broken. However, he had been bleeding badly from the wound. Had Zachariah not been there at the right time, it's possible that Mohamed might have bled out. Ever since this incident, Zachariah always likes to remind Mohamed—and everyone else—that he helped save Mohamed's life.

I was glad to hear of the fortuitous outcome, but Mohamed's injury confirmed my deepest fears. Mogadishu was as it always had been for as long as I'd remembered: an unsafe place that could kill you without warning.

The actions of the Al Shabaab terrorists gave further credence to my assumption. On December 3, 2009, they carried out one of the most shocking massacres in Somalia at Hotel Shamo. A suicide bomber went into a graduation ceremony for medical students and detonated himself. The explosion killed twenty-five people, including three ministers of the Transitional Federal Government. It injured sixty more. Among the dead and wounded were students, their parents, and professors from Benadir University, as well as government officials.

However, the attack at Hotel Shamo marked a turning point. The people of Somalia had had enough of Al Shabaab's ruthless killings. But it wouldn't be until August 2011 that Al Shabaab began removing themselves from Mogadishu under the auspices of "a change in tactics." What this ultimately meant is that they would no longer fight face-to-face. Now they'd "fight" just as they'd done at Hotel Shamo: via suicide bombers.

Even though the threat of terrorism was never fully removed from Somalia, the withdrawal of Al Shabaab from Mogadishu was a welcome sign. Residents returned to their homes, including my parents. My father's house had survived, but my mother's house had incurred a great amount of damage. It would need a new roof, new windows, new doors, and more.

When I heard about the state of her house, all I could think was, *You don't have to live there.*

But my mother is a strong-willed, determined woman.

I know that to be true because she had helped raise a strong-willed, determined son.

14 Family Is Family

While my family in Somalia endured hard times pressed upon them by the country's constant chaos, my family in America suffered through difficulties of a different sort. In May 2007, my sister Luul and her son, Bilal, moved from Somalia and back to America to stay with me. She moved for the same reason any Somali would have moved at that time: just to get her family safely out of Mogadishu. But I had a hunch she was also moving for the same reason I had: there were opportunities in America that existed nowhere else. And while I needed physical help, Luul would need something wholly different.

At the time, I was living in a one-bedroom apartment in Roswell, Georgia. With a month left on my lease, I asked my cousin Amina if Luul and her son could stay with her. Amina, ever-helpful, obliged my request. Once that month had passed, I rented a larger, two-bedroom apartment in Clarkston and moved in with my sister and nephew. I chose Clarkston mainly because a large number of Somalis already lived there. The town even had a Somali shopping mall complete with restaurants, groceries, and clothing stores. I knew adjusting to life in America would be easier for Luul in a place like Clarkston.

But I only knew a little about the real adjustment Luul was having to make. Instead of battling the sometimes-bewildering world of 21st-century America, my sister was fighting bipolar depression. This would become our joint personal war for the next five years.

Once we had settled ourselves into the new apartment, I deftly tried to bring up her emotional instability.

"Luul, I think you need to see a psychiatrist or therapist. I think it would help you."

"Abdi, I'm OK."

I let my silence speak my thoughts for me.

"I'm *OK*, Abdi. It's everyone else who's after me."

Now, I'm not a psychiatrist, but even I knew something was off with that statement. I didn't press the issue then. It seemed that every time I brought up the issue of her depression, she became annoyed with me.

We were further constrained by three unfortunate realities: she didn't have health insurance yet; I couldn't afford taking her to a private practice; and she wouldn't visit a public clinic. With no qualified help on the horizon, her problems increased while her health deteriorated. After two weeks of seeing her like that, I didn't know what to do, so I went to my last resort.

———

Had she known what I was doing, I'm sure she would have immediately left the apartment and taken Bilal with her.

As soon as Luul saw the ambulance outside of the apartment, she locked herself inside her room. I imagine that she had to have heard my conversation with the EMT.

He asked, "What's wrong here?"

"It's my sister. I think she's having a psychotic episode. She's been talking excessively, and she hasn't been sleeping well. She's agitated and irritable. Furthermore, she hasn't been taking any medications, so her condition has been worsening."

"Do you believe she's a threat to herself or others?"

I nodded. "Possibly." I meant it.

My female cousin tried to persuade Luul to come out by telling her she would see a doctor at the hospital and she would be back home soon.

Luul eventually came out. The EMT escorted her to the ambulance, and the ambulance escorted her to DeKalb Medical Center. I followed the ambulance to the ER.

When I next saw her, she wouldn't look at me or talk to me. She was fuming.

A nurse had taken her blood, and other staff had asked her questions. Though we'd arrived in the early evening, it wasn't until near midnight that she was admitted to the psychiatric section.

I stayed in the ER's waiting room the entire time, sometimes answering questions from medical staff who were looking for the same answers I wish I'd had. I was exhausted, but I didn't want to leave without seeing to it that Luul was getting the right kind of treatment. And, knowing how upset she was with me, I certainly couldn't leave without saying good-bye. I asked a nurse which room my sister was in. The nurse led the way.

As soon as I wheeled into her room, my sister forcibly turned her head away from me.

"Hi, Luul," I said rather meekly. I felt bad for what I'd done, but not bad enough to regret it. "How are you feeling now?"

She slowly turned back around to face me. "I never want to see you again." A mixture of anger and sadness caused her voice to falter. "Don't ever come back."

I felt as if a knife had been plunged into my heart at the same moment I'd been struck by lightning. I couldn't believe what I was hearing. Was she serious? I was shocked, and I feared that she meant what she said. Instead of pleading my case, I wordlessly wheeled myself out of her room.

With my thoughts racing and my emotions about to flood my eyes, I rolled to the parking deck, into the elevator, down to where I'd parked, and moved myself into my car. Then, within the safe and private confines of my car, my emotional floodgates swung wide.

Why? Why? Why!? Why am I in this terrible situation? I have my own health challenges to deal with! And I'm constantly worried about my parents and family in Somalia. And I feel like I just work all the time, and all my money goes to family. And now this? This is my repayment for trying to help my sister? This is too much to bear. And wouldn't people understand if I just didn't help?

Once those momentary, terrible thoughts were released, my more rational and loving side chimed in: *Maybe you've been put in this position to test your limits—again. You can overcome this challenge. Just consider how many you've overcome so far. You have to realize, Abdi: your family's struggles are your struggles too, whether they're eight thousand miles away or in the room right next to yours. Family is family. And you know this to be true too: suffering together far outweighs suffering alone.*

For a rare moment, I let myself feel sorry for myself, but then I wiped away the tears and committed myself toward taking care of Luul and Bilal as best as I could.

She wouldn't be able to get rid of me that easily.

A few days following her admission to DeKalb, my sister was transferred to Georgia Regional Hospital in Decatur, which specialized in treating those diagnosed with bipolar depression. She was given medicine to stabilize her moods, though she thought them ineffective. However, I noticed a change and was glad she was finally receiving proper help.

I visited her a couple of times a week while she was at Georgia Regional. As amends for calling 911, I made sure to bring her good food every time I visited. She didn't particularly like what the hospital had been giving her. Even though she was still uneasy with me and our relationship had taken a beating, she slowly came to understand why I'd done what I did. She was discharged after a two-week stay. We went back home to Clarkston, and Luul was reunited with her deep source of joy and peace: her son, Bilal.

Over the next five-and-a-half years, my sister would have periodic psychotic episodes. I never had to call 911 again, but her episodes did sometimes make me fear being physically harmed. More than that, I felt emotionally hurt after her outbursts. Whenever she felt normal, she was kind and caring. But whenever her mood severely swung the other way, she became hateful, and it seemed like she hated me the most. In hindsight, it's probably because I was just the nearest target within her blast radius. However, she would often come back after settling down and would ask me to forgive her for her angry outbursts. That's when the kind Luul would shine like a sun through her bipolar cloud.

She would blame me for her pain, despite the fact that I was the one doing my best to help her. I took her to her doctors' appointments. I stayed with her at those appointments to ensure that the doctors could get a fair picture of her mental state. And I would constantly ask if she had been taking her medicine. On the good days, she was grateful for my care. She was the happy Luul I'd known from years ago. But on the bad days, she wanted me gone, or she wanted to leave.

I understood what it was like to lose hope when everything seemed to be going against you. I was empathetic toward my sister's plight, even though I knew I couldn't fully understand what she was fighting internally. But my support never wavered, and I never doubted my commitment to her after that self-pitying moment in the car. I chose to believe in the hope of tomorrow. I chose to believe what had proven true in my life over and over: things *will* get better.

Still, as any caretaker of a family member knows, the requirements of time and emotion can drain you. When you pair that weight with the necessary burden of a full-time job, then multiply those responsibilities by your own physical limitations, something has to give, either by choice or by default. For me, what gave was our location.

Even though I felt like I'd been walking a tightrope between my job responsibilities and my family responsibilities, I'd done steady work for AT&T, which proved helpful. Luul's therapy in Atlanta wasn't working well, and she'd had an excellent psychiatric doctor when we'd lived in Raleigh, North Carolina. I felt as if I were barely holding our lives together in Atlanta. To consider splitting time between Raleigh and Atlanta—a distance of four hundred miles—seemed preposterous. But because I wanted my sister to get well, I asked AT&T for a relocation. They obliged, and on June 29, 2009, our strange family of three moved back to Raleigh.

I located an AT&T office ten minutes from our new apartment and inquired about an available cube. There were plenty, and I began working at that office. My family's troubles at home and abroad had negatively affected my career. I didn't ask for additional work assignments or promotions because I knew I couldn't handle the added responsibilities back then, even though the extra income surely would have been helpful. But, as in so many other areas of my life, I didn't make excuses. I took pride in my work and did the best I could. I was grateful for my job. My position with AT&T meant a lot to me—and my family.

In May 2012, Luul was approved to live in a subsidized apartment for low-income families. She and Bilal moved out that month. She adjusted well. Her son—a great kid whom I love very much—continued his education. My role was to sometimes schedule doctors' appointments for her and help with grocery shopping. Compared to where she was, I was relieved to see my sister living in her own place with minimal assistance. She has come a long way. Things *did* get better. *And* she still talks to me

I moved out of the apartment we shared and into a one-bedroom apartment near Cary, North Carolina. After more than five years of shouldering the caretaking of a family member with a mental illness, I was ready to pull my life together. For the next two years, I refocused my efforts on my job.

Then, in 2014, a once-in-my-lifetime opportunity presented itself that I couldn't resist.

I got to go home.

15 You Can Go Home Again

The last time I'd seen my mother was January 1994. Twenty years later, I finally had the means and the opportunity to return to my homeland to see her, as well as my father (whom I hadn't seen since 2002), my sisters, and my many relatives back in Mogadishu. While the city was still dangerous, to a degree, it was likely as safe as it was going to get. My parents cautioned me against coming, but I relayed that I'd be arriving regardless of how difficult or risky the trip would be. Plus, I feared that if I didn't make the journey, my parents may pass away before I'd get to see them again.

On January 22, 2014, I embarked on that two-day trip by myself. On a frigid day, I departed from the JFK airport in New York City on Turkish Airlines—a flight I almost missed. After a nine-hour flight to Istanbul, I had a layover of six hours. All I thought about during those hours was how much I wanted to see my parents. I wondered how my mother would look after twenty years. Would she seem old or frail or skinny yet healthy? I also wondered how I'd look to her! Much had changed for the both of us within the last two decades. I boarded the next leg of my flight, from Istanbul to Mogadishu, with great anticipation.

Upon landing at Aden Ade International Airport in Mogadishu, two employees spotted me and my predicament after all of the other passengers had departed the plane. Unlike most international airports, Aden Ade didn't have a docking tarmac, which meant I'd need help to disembark. These employees located my wheelchair, placed it next to the long staircase by the plane's exit, then walked back to me. "We're here to carry you to your wheelchair, Sir." I gratefully accepted their help and was refreshed by their hospitality. I was also reminded of a fact that was seldom if ever portrayed on American TV: most Somalis are good people.

Once inside the airport, a man who looked vaguely familiar approached me. "Is this Abdi? Are you my cousin?"

"Is this Ahmed?" I'd prearranged transportation from the airport to my parents' houses so they wouldn't have to worry about coming to get me. However, I hadn't seen this cousin in twenty years! In fact, I hadn't known him all that well even when I'd lived in Somalia. Part of me wondered if he were actually family.

Ahmed replied affirmatively, and then he hugged me. He was definitely family.

He took me to a VIP section of the airport where I paid fifty dollars for a visa—to be allowed back into the country of my birth. But, since I was a US citizen, it was a requirement I gladly paid. After paying my government a pittance to be temporarily readmitted to my homeland, I asked Ahmed where his car was.

"I am going to call a taxi for you, Abdi. As a government employee, we're often targeted by Al Shabaab, so I cannot go further into the city with you. It would not be safe."

I should have known. Mogadishu was still Mogadishu. Nothing was easy here—not even getting a ride home.

———

I called my mom from the airport to tell her that I'd landed safely on Somalia's shores and I'd be seeing her soon. She was overjoyed to hear my voice, as I was hers. The last time we'd talked was just prior to my departure from Raleigh for that trip, but our close physical proximity coupled with the fact that we were soon to see each other was making me emotional. I was anxious to get out of the airport and into town.

My taxi driver headed toward my parents' homes in the Suuqa Hoolaha neighborhood in the northernmost part of Mogadishu. On the twenty-minute ride, which felt like two hours, I saw how different Mogadishu had become. The city seemed to be slowly coming back to life. We passed so much construction that I was amazed. New buildings were going up all over, and it seemed that many older buildings were in the midst of remodels. For the first time in a long time, a sense of optimism seemed to be rising alongside every new building. Maybe the people of Mogadishu were feeling the effects of real, lasting peace.

To test my hypothesis, I asked my cab driver about the city and his views of its future. He corroborated my assumptions: he was upbeat and bullish about what lay ahead for Mogadishu and Somalia. He reminded me of the warring factions that had been a daily part of regular living in Somalia for the last two decades. Unbeknownst to him, as he spoke about the destruction of the city and how some neighborhoods still had few standing structures, he brought images back to my mind of bombed-out buildings and freshly dead corpses.

I shook my head to remove those thoughts. The past was the past. It could stay there.

Then he relayed a shocking fact to me. Mogadishu's property values had skyrocketed. Some houses were selling for a million dollars, an unheard-of sum. Even ordinary houses had been selling for over a hundred thousand dollars. I asked him how such prices were possible. He relayed that there was excessive money in our market and how Somalis returning from our civil-war diaspora had been pouring millions of dollars into the city in the hopes of making a quick and substantial profit. Apparently, it was working. He said that many profiteers had bought acres of land on the cheap and then sold them a few months later for three to five times as much as they'd paid. But, just as we pulled into the Suuqa Hoolaha market, he said that property values had fallen recently, and it seemed like the market was currently frozen.

Before exiting his car, I asked the driver if I could use his phone to call my father, who was supposed to have been waiting for me in the market.

My parents lived in separate houses, and neither of them had had those houses when I'd last lived in Somalia. I wouldn't have known where to go unless someone led me there.

The driver agreed and offered his phone. As I was calling my father, I peered out of the window and saw his unmistakable shape standing on the other side of the road from us. The driver pulled closer to him.

I looked at my dad through the window. Despite myself, I thought, *Wow. He looks* much *older.* I hadn't seen him for twelve years! I imagine I might have looked much older to him too. As I was lost in wonder at finally getting to see my dad again, my nephews Bilal and Abdirahman, who were eleven and twelve, respectively, rushed to the taxi. They were so excited to see me that they hugged me through the taxi's window.

My father went around to the other side of the car and climbed into the backseat. My nephews ran ahead of us to my mother's house, which wasn't far down the main street we were on. I hugged and kissed my father. He smiled and directed the driver toward my mother's house.

Nothing felt real, but everything felt right.

I was home and both of my parents were still alive.

Coming from Mogadishu, not everyone could say that.

The driver pulled up to the gate at my mother's house. My father and I extricated ourselves from the car and walked inside. In what felt like just a moment and a yet a lifetime, there she was: my beautiful mother, whom I'd dearly missed ever since having to say good-bye to her twenty years before.

I hugged and kissed her, then kissed her some more. I couldn't believe my mother was standing in front of me! She couldn't believe I was sitting in front of her. My mom had suffered a lot. She'd lost her beloved daughter, Ureeji. She had stayed in Mogadishu for most of the civil war. She looked tired. At sixty-eight, my mom had been the bedrock of our family. She never complained about anything in her life. At times, I felt as if I were dreaming. It was unreal to be with my mother. Our reunion felt a world away and beyond my reach, but here she was in front of me.

"Mom, you look older and skinnier than I imagined."

She replied, "I am happy to see you, my son."

She was thankful for us to reunite. Nothing else was important that day.

I hugged my sisters, Luul and Halima. Then my mother introduced me to Ureeji's children. Since Ureeji's death, these four boys and one girl had lived with my mother. In other words, she was their grandmother by definition, but she was now their mother by default. She was also, in effect, their father. Shortly after Ureeji's passing, her husband had immigrated to London to seek an opportunity that would better the future of his kids. He loved his kids and supported them financially.

But during those moments hugging my family, the world shrank to the size of our foyer. Our collective history faded into the past. We had each other in the present moment. I was overjoyed. I didn't want the moment to end.

But such happiness isn't sustainable—particularly in Mogadishu.

For most of my two weeks in the city at my mother's house, my mother was sickly. She'd struggled with asthma and diabetes for years, but she was a true mother. She had always sacrificed her own health so that she could care to the needs of others. Even through the trials and tribulations she endured, she seldom if ever sought help for herself.

So I was grateful to offer my assistance during my stay. I remember one series of events that was indicative of Somalia's medical processes. We took a taxi to see her local doctor, but he was so busy that his office had run out of the numbers they hand out for people waiting to be seen. They turned us away and told us to come back the next day.

I didn't want to wait, so we went next door, where another doctor with a similar practice resided. That doctor wasn't in, but a colleague of his was. When I asked who the available physician was, she pointed to a young man in blue jeans and a white coat.

I raised my eye at her. "Him?"

She nodded, understanding the look of doubt that had spread across my face. "He has multiple degrees from America."

She thought she was being reassuring, but her words enhanced my doubt. *If he received his medical degree in America, why did he leave America!? He could have earned a gazillion times more money there than here in Mogadishu.*

I thought back to all of my dealings with doctors and nurses and medical personnel when I was younger. In Somalia, there was no such thing as governmental regulations on the medical industry. Certifications weren't necessary to be a doctor. No medical boards existed to ensure that a doctor actually had a doctorate. From my perspective, anyone with a minimal understanding of medicine—and a white lab coat—could open their own practice and begin seeing (paying) clients. Furthermore, most practices had their own pharmacies, which clients were recommended to use by the owner-doctor.

It seemed like some things—still—hadn't changed.

I motioned for my mother to bend down so I could whisper in her ear. "I'm not comfortable with you seeing Dr. Blue Jeans."

Ever the patient one, my mom just replied, "Let's just wait and see."

After her checkup, we were referred to an X-ray lab near the airport, and we left immediately for that lab. One of my nephews came with us. On our arrival there, we noticed a long line. Sure enough, we were number eighty-nine.

We waited so long that we witnessed a frail senior adult being brought out on a stretcher and leaned against a tree close to where we were waiting. In what seemed like just a few moments later, lab staff rushed back out to the man and began attempts at resuscitation. But their efforts failed. The man was declared dead on the spot. I couldn't believe my eyes.

Soon after that shocking and surreal moment, the lab techs called out,

"Eighty-nine!" But, because my mother, my nephew, and I were in different parts of the building, we couldn't get to the X-ray room fast enough. When we got to the room we all needed to get to, the tech called out, "Ninety!"

I wheeled in front of the man. "Wait a minute! You called us, eighty-nine. Why are you calling the next number already? Isn't there a fairness?"

"Where have you seen fairness in Mogadishu?"

His reply enraged me and relegated me to speechlessness. But I couldn't argue his logic. Not here, and not given what he'd likely seen as part of his job.

Fortunately, he let us in as soon as number ninety was finished. We received the necessary X-rays a few minutes later, then we were on our way back to Dr. Blue Jeans. When we arrived, Dr. Blue Jeans was just about to leave. Thankfully, he briefly reviewed my mother's X-rays, and then referred us to yet another doctor—who just so happened to be the first doctor we'd tried to see earlier that day.

Through further tests, including another trip to yet another medical testing facility, my mother was diagnosed with tuberculosis. She was given a prescription, which we promptly filled before finally returning home. Even though her diagnosis wasn't great, at least we now knew what we were dealing with.

Per the doctor's orders, we moved my late sister's two youngest children to their paternal grandmother's house. Since they were still relatively young then, they were more susceptible to contracting tuberculosis, particularly because the virus spreads easily by sharing cups and spoons—not to mention, these two children slept in my mother's room. Consequently, for the remaining duration of my stay and my mother's recuperation, those two children stayed with their other grandmother.

When I wasn't focused on my mother's health, I relished the opportunity to reconnect with my father and dozens of relatives I hadn't seen in two decades. Some I didn't even recognize until they told me their names.

One day, my father told me that his reading of the Qur'an had become less clear. So I took him to an eyecare doctor near the flower bar in Mogadishu. On our way to the doctor's office, the cab driver told us that the residents in the city center hadn't sleep last night. We asked why. He replied that it was because unpaid soldiers had wanted to send a message to the president that they better be paid or else. In reality, these were likely ghost soldiers who only existed on papers that some officers used to collect large sums of money to enrich themselves. So we asked who shelled the city then. His response was a bit shocking: "It only took a handful of paid rogue actors to shell the city from all four corners—enough to cause mayhem to force residents to demand the government pay the supposedly protesting solders."

We got to the doctor's office. My father's eyes were examined, and he was prescribed reading glasses. We bought them at the practice and left for home.

But the two people I truly wanted to see most (after my parents) weren't there: my dear sister, Ureeji, whom I'd last seen at Aden Ade airport twenty years ago and whose support had made possible my quest for a better life, and my uncle—my mother's brother who'd warned us to stay with him on that fateful night in Mogadishu—who had passed away the year before. When I remembered him, all I could see was the caring, compassionate man I'd known as a child. My mother would later tell me that she had pledged to look after the family he'd left behind. I felt it was my duty to likewise pledge my support to them as well. He had done so much for us—for me—that I owed him at least that much, if not much, much more.

———————

My two-week Mogadishu "vacation" ended far sooner than I wanted it to, but not without warning me, yet again, of why I'd left.

On an uneventful day, while heading back to my mother's house in a cab, we got stuck in a traffic jam. This was not unusual. Neither were the governmental checkpoints. Unfortunately, on this day, truck drivers were protesting the fees they were required to pay at these checkpoints. Consequently, the drivers had purposefully blocked the main road from Mogadishu to Afgoye.

We were stuck on that road, totally immobile—a situation I knew all too well.

The driver began to explain the situation to us. "You do know it's dangerous to be stuck in traffic in Mogadishu?"

I nodded, curious as to whether this driver thought he was lessening our fear.

He kept talking. "If a government convoy came through here right now, they'd shoot their way out. If you're stuck in front of one, you'd better pull over to the side. If you can't pull over, you'd better get out of the car and take cover."

As soon as he'd said that, a pickup truck with armed guards appeared in the distance. They were driving straight toward us.

I glanced outside. At least our car was already to the side of the road. But we were so far to the side that I saw my archnemesis waiting to consume me. If we had to flee the car—and I were able to somehow get my wheelchair and myself onto my chair—my wheels would be instantly eaten by the all-consuming sand. Then I'd be shot—a sitting duck.

As these fears swirled through my mind, the driver pointed to the rapidly oncoming trucks. "That's an official convoy. Let's hope and pray they don't shoot their way out."

I hoped and I prayed.

The trucks passed us on the opposite side of the road.

Multiple sighs of relief escaped our car.

It was right about then that I thought, *Maybe it's time I went back home, back to the US.*

16 The Conversation I Didn't Want to End

Even though I was ready to go back to America, fate had other plans. But this time, they were excellent plans.

A few days before I was set to depart Mogadishu, my older cousin Adar told me she knew a young lady whom she wanted me to meet. I raised an eyebrow toward her and just said, "OK." I didn't ask further questions. In fact, I wasn't sure I'd even be able to meet this woman because of my schedule. Trying to get out of the country was just as much of a hassle as trying to get into it. The more time you can give yourself to prepare for the inevitable obstacles, the better.

But, as a thirty-five-year-old man who hadn't dated much (because I'd been focused on my job and taking care of my family, both in the US and in Somalia) and who someday wanted a family, I was intrigued by the possibility. I hoped I could make our meeting. I told my cousin, "I'll see you Wednesday around one."

A few days later, I arrived at my cousin's villa. Once I was seated at her table, my cousin brought me a blended fruit juice, which I gladly accepted. Then she left back into her house. Another cousin then promptly spilled his drink on the table, some of which splashed onto my T-shirt and pants. He apologized. I said, "No problem."

Had I known what was about to happen, I would have thought it was a bigger problem.

As I tried to clean myself, Adar returned and asked me to follow her to a room with a beautiful sofa.

"Abdi, I'd like to introduce you to Shankaron." As I looked at her, I thought, *Wow—this is a dazzling woman.*

Doing my best to cover up the recent stains on my clothing, I'm sure I offered Shankaron a goofy smile.

Adar smiled at me as she departed, leaving Shankaron and me alone.

For the next fifteen minutes, we got to know each other. It was neither a long nor a deep conversation, but, by its end, I knew one thing: I wanted to talk with this woman for the rest of my life.

I greeted her customarily. "Aslamu Alaikum." (Peace be on to you.)

Softly, she replied, "Wa'alaikum–salaam." (And unto you peace.)

"How are you doing? How is your family doing?"

I was afraid that we might not connect well since I felt our age gap was as wide as the ocean. I was thirty-five; she was nineteen. However, she was much wiser and more confident than her age suggested. I really liked her smile; it was contagious. We connected really well from the start of our conversation. I felt I could talk with her for hours.

She asked me why I was in Mogadishu. I told her I was visiting my parents.

Since there was a beautiful wall-to-wall sofa seat, I transferred from my wheelchair to the seat. Before we said good-bye, I asked if she could hold my wheelchair for me.

Without hesitation, she said, "Of course." She held on to it for me and asked if I needed any help getting onto the wheelchair, to which I replied, "I am fine. Thanks!"

That small gesture gave me a glimpse into her humanity and left me feeling that she's really a great person.

"Shankaron, I will be traveling back to the United States in two days. Do you think we could still keep this conversation going?"

She smiled her reply. "Yes, of course."

I'd say I felt weak in the knees, but that saying means nothing to me. All I knew is that whatever I felt, I didn't want it to end. The longer we sat together, the harder it was getting for me to leave Somalia.

Knowing that she couldn't stay long, we said our good-byes and Shankaron left.

As soon as she saw her friend leaving, Adar returned to the room. "What did you think of her?"

"She's *fantastic*."

Adar smiled wide. "I know. And I knew you two would like each other. I just had a feeling."

"Thank you for introducing us, cousin."

After leaving Adar's house, I couldn't help but talk about Shankaron. I told my father about the short date, and, ever the practical man who knew his son too well, he asked, "You're leaving Friday morning, right? She is here. You are leaving. How is that going to work out?"

"If we have a relationship across the Atlantic?"

"Yes."

"I don't know."

"I don't know either." My father paused. "Are you planning to come back? If not, are you planning to apply for a visa for someone you don't know anything about? And what about your job prospects?"

"I don't know, Dad. But she's the woman I've been waiting for. It's going to work out one way or the other."

He patted my shoulder. I saw a half-smile escape his face. I could tell that he could tell I was lovestruck.

I had a strong feeling that, in due time, Shankaron and I would be together as husband and wife. No distance nor challenges would deter me.

I called Shankaron that night as well as the following night. She wished me safe travels back to the US. I reaffirmed my commitment to stay in touch with her.

I flew out of Mogadishu on Friday, February 7, 2014. We wouldn't be officially married until September 14, 2014, and, due to the laborious and time-consuming immigration process, we wouldn't live together as husband and wife in America until January 30, 2016.

If I would have known I'd have to wait two years to have my wife with me full-time, would I have made the same decisions?

Absolutely.

———————

Of course, departing Somalia was difficult, and not just because I was leaving Shankaron and I knew there was a great possibility I may never see my parents again. Leaving the country was practically difficult. Of all the days that I could have chosen to leave, I chose Friday, February 7, 2014: the same day that my Turkish Airlines flight was bringing home the body of the recently deceased former Prime Minister, Abdirizak Hajji Hussein, one of Somalia's most beloved figures.

When substantial events like this happened, the city of Mogadishu went on lockdown. Because high-level dignitaries were scheduled to attend the Prime Minister's ceremony, threats of terrorism increased exponentially. The city apparently knew of no other way to police itself during these events other than to lock down a million people.

Of course, the ceremony was scheduled to take place at Aden Ade International Airport, the same airport I needed to depart from that morning. And I couldn't miss that flight. My livelihood and the continued financial support of my family depended on me making that flight.

You see, a few days prior to when I'd left for Somalia, I'd been told by my boss at AT&T that there was a chance I'd be included in a workforce reduction. That was nice business-talk for, "You may be let go while you're on vacation." She asked for a phone number where I could be reached during my vacation, and I gave her my mother's number.

I replied, "I don't wish to get a call from you, but if I do, I'll understand." It was an awkward conversation, and part of me wanted to tell my boss exactly how much of my life and my family's lives depended on *my* job. But I'm not one to complain or to make my problems other people's problems. She was just doing her job, and I could tell that she wasn't enjoying this aspect of it.

Sure enough, I received a call from her at my mother's house during the second week of my stay.

Knowing that we both knew why she was calling, she got straight to the point. "Abdi, I'm sorry to say that your position has been eliminated. Your employment with AT&T will end on March 31, 2014—unless you receive another offer from within the company."

Even though I knew what she was going to tell me as soon as she'd told me her name, hearing the actual words—"your position has been eliminated"—was devastating. I briefly took in the irony that I received that news in my mother's house, a place that some of my earnings had gone into.

"Are you there, Abdi?"

I guess I'd been quiet for too long.

"Yes. I'm just digesting this news."

"I'm sorry, Abdi." She paused. "When will you be coming back to the US?"

"My arrival flight is scheduled for Saturday, February 8, and I'll be back in the office on Monday, February 10."

"I know this is not the kind of news you want to hear while on your vacation. Let's talk more when you get back. I will call you on the tenth."

"OK. Thank you."

"Despite this call, I hope you have a great rest of your vacation."

"OK. Thank you."

We hung up. Because they'd heard my end of it and saw how my demeanor had drastically changed during the call, my mother and nephews immediately asked me about what had just happened.

"It was just a work call." I didn't offer the full truth at first because I didn't want my mother to worry and I didn't want to cast a somber mood over our happy times.

My mother knew I wasn't telling the whole truth and prodded me to know more.

"My position has been eliminated." I paused and looked up at my mom, knowing what she may have been thinking. "But don't worry. I will find a better job than the one I lost."

The following day, I told my father about what had transpired and likewise reassured him that I'd find an even better job. They weren't hollow words either. I truly believed a better opportunity awaited me once I returned to America. By the time I had absorbed the news that my former job was no longer mine, I had little sorrow for its loss.

Plus, as I rode to the airport on my final day in Somalia, I reflected on my trip. I'd hugged my mother, whom I hadn't seen in twenty years. I'd talked face-to-face with my father, whom I hadn't seen in twelve years. I'd reconnected with siblings and cousins, some of whom I hadn't seen in years and others I'd never met.

And I'd met Shankaron.

The trip had been magical—until the day I had to leave.

Knowing that I was scheduled for a cab ride to the airport early that morning, the driver called me at 5:30 a.m. "The city's on lockdown for the prime minister's ceremony today."

"What can we do?" I asked. By now, this cab driver and I had developed a good rapport. He was the same driver who'd taken me around Mogadishu for the duration of my two-week stay.

He replied, "I don't know if there is anything we can do to get to the airport today. Once the city is locked down, the streets and shopping malls are all completely closed. And troop-heavy government checkpoints are set up all over the city."

"I understand. Come get me in an hour anyways."

"OK. It's your money."

Knowing that I couldn't miss my flight, I called my cousin Ahmed, the government official who'd met me at the airport when I had arrived. Maybe he could help get me to the airport today.

"I'm sorry, Abdi. The city's on lockdown. Unless you're someone of high rank, you're not getting into or out of the city. You might as well reschedule your flight."

"Thanks, Ahmed." I was not thankful.

My driver arrived at 6:00 a.m. My takeoff was at 10:30 a.m. We had four-and-a-half hours to traverse twenty miles while the city was on lockdown.

As I told my family good-bye, I said, "I hope to be back sooner than another twenty years." They laughed and wished me well—and particularly with getting through the checkpoints.

The driver hit the gas and we were off. I knew he doubted we'd get very far, but I also knew that he wanted to make at least some money on a day when he likely wouldn't have made any. However, I wanted to prove his doubts wrong. I wanted to show him the power of positive thinking. I wanted to show him that I could convince the checkpoint soldiers to let us through. I was given that opportunity less than three miles away from my mother's house.

Noticeably armed with AK-47s, soldiers from the Somali National Army stopped us. "Turn back now."

The driver pled with them to let us pass. He turned to me and said, "Abdi, they're not going to let us through."

I pondered our possibilities for a second, then Ahmed's words came to mind: *Unless you're someone of high rank, you're not getting into or out of the city.* "Tell them I was invited to the ceremony and can't miss such an important event."

My driver smiled at me, then turned around and played it cool with the solider.

The soldier replied, "Let me talk to my commander." He left but returned quickly. "You're clear to go through."

As soon as we were far enough away from the checkpoint, the driver looked at me and grinned. But his smile faded when we hit the next checkpoint less than a mile away.

Before pulling up to these soldiers, I nodded at my driver, intimating that he should try the same approach.

It worked.

After that checkpoint, my driver—now fully complicit in this daring adventure—took backroads throughout Mogadishu. He knew the city very well and somehow managed to evade every checkpoint after those first two.

I called my cousin Ahmed and told him to expect me at the airport.

"What!? You made it through? How?"

"I thought you knew that I was someone of high rank who's expected at the ceremony."

He laughed. "OK, King Abdi. I will see you at the airport's entrance."

We arrived at the airport without further delay. It was 7:30 a.m. My cousin carried my luggage through the screening area for me, saving me precious minutes and likely some hassle. He got me to the departure terminal because he knew a lot of people at the airport. Shortly after, he left.

The governmental ceremony was about to conclude. Somali president Hassan Sheikh Mohamud, Prime Minister Abdiweli Sheikh Ahmed, and Speaker of Parliament Mohamed Osman Jawari were there, as well as other dignitaries, to receive the casket and pay their respects to the deceased prime minister. A lot of security personnel were inside and outside of the airport. However, there were a handful of people inside the departure terminal, including me. Through glass windows, we watched as the ceremony concluded a few feet outside of the waiting area.

I have a lot of respect for what Prime Minister Abdirazak stood for. He was above the tribal politics. He was well respected and a true statesman.

We had to wait until it was over before boarding the plane.

But I got on that plane on a day when no one believed I would. I felt triumphant, as if nothing could stop me.

Then I remembered: I'm heading home to a job that will end in less than two months, and I'm leaving my future wife in Somalia.

Both of those circumstances need to change.

17 RDU > DFW > LHR > NBO > MBA

When I finally arrived back at my home in Raleigh, everything seemed frozen in time. The kitchen looked exactly as I'd left it—messy. I couldn't believe I'd only been gone for two weeks. It had felt like months. And when I thought about Shankaron, it felt like far too much time had elapsed since last I'd seen her, even though it had only been a few days since our first and only meeting. I knew that if I wanted her to be part of my life, I would have to take care of my most pressing need first: securing a new job. Only after I leaped that hurdle could I even begin to think about what was next: seeing Shankaron again, wooing her to become closer to me, asking her to marry me, and then, finally, initiating the process to have her immigrate to the United States.

I hesitated to think about all of those steps at the same time because, collectively, they were too great a burden to bear. So I did what I'd done for most of my life: I figured out the next step I had to take, then took it.

Fortunately, my steps were often aided by outside influences who wanted to help me along the way. For instance, when I returned to work on Monday, February 10, 2014, knowing that I had less than two months at that job, a surprising email awaited me. Charlotte, now a former AT&T employee I'd known since she had interviewed me for the Cingular job on the NCSU campus in 2005 and whom I considered a mentor, asked if I'd been impacted by the recent round of layoffs. I immediately replied in the affirmative and asked if she could help me land another position within the company. She said yes.

Over the next few days and per Charlotte's suggestions, I updated my long-dormant resume to reflect the accomplishments I'd achieved, the skills I'd learned, and the qualifications I'd gained since being employed by AT&T for the past eight years. Charlotte and I also had a number of conversations by phone.

She asked, "What kinds of jobs are you interested in?"

I replied, "Any sales operations or corporate support positions that I'm qualified for."

"And are you willing to relocate?"

"Yes." I paused. "But just not to Alaska. I am severely allergic to snow!"

She laughed. "I don't think that'll be a problem, Abdi. But that's good to know."

In addition to Charlotte's assistance and insight, I also reached out to my previous bosses, including Judy. She'd been my manager when I'd managed the Virtual Sales Channel after "graduating" from the B2B Sales program. She put her full support behind me staying with the company in another position and dedicated many hours toward writing recommendation letters on my behalf, which she sent directly to the hiring managers of those positions. We even had weekly calls to discuss my progress. Furthermore, she had also encouraged her team to support me in any way possible, which was a tremendous help.

Through this process, I became chiefly interested in two positions, both based in Atlanta. Even though I'd said I was open to relocating, I knew I would feel more at ease if I could live somewhere familiar. However, after interviewing for both positions, neither one materialized into an offer. I was momentarily dejected, but I knew more opportunities within the company awaited me.

Then, on Friday afternoon, February 14, Charlotte emailed me: an AT&T executive was looking to fill a position in his Business Markets Pricing group. She thought I'd be a good fit, so I called her to get more information. To my surprise, she relayed that the hiring executive may want to talk to me *that day*. He and I would have a call at 7 p.m. that night.

Everything about the job sounded great—until he asked me a question I'd recently heard before.

"Mr. Warsame, are you willing to relocate to Atlanta or Dallas for this position? To be honest, I'm looking for someone for our Dallas office."

I paused, and I sensed that he discerned my hesitation. But I didn't want to squander such an opportunity, especially after Charlotte and Judy and so many other people had devoted their time and efforts toward ensuring my continued employment at AT&T. "May I have the weekend to consider your question? I'll let you know my decision first thing Monday morning."

He graciously agreed to give me the weekend.

That following Monday, I emailed Mr. Reid. "I would like to accept the offer of employment . . . in Dallas."

Although I think I could have pressed to relocate to Atlanta, a place that I knew and in which I felt more comfortable, I ultimately chose Dallas for two reasons: that's where Mr. Reid and AT&T's corporate headquarters are located. I figured that my opportunities for continued advancement within the company might be better if I were stationed at its home base—an assumption that has proven itself true.

I started working in my new role on April 1, 2014, while still living in Raleigh. I moved to Irving, Texas, on May 31, 2014, into a wheelchair-accessible apartment that was fifteen miles away from my office at the AT&T headquarters. My hiring manager didn't know about my disability until I rolled into his office on June 5, 2014. I didn't tell him about my disability during the hiring process because it didn't matter.

Prior to moving, I'd gotten in touch with my good friend since 2006, Yusuf. Back then, he had relocated to Atlanta from Dallas at the same time I'd relocated from Raleigh to Atlanta. In addition to our plight as recent implants to Atlanta, we were also both from Mogadishu. When we met in an Alpharetta mosque, we immediately clicked and formed a strong brotherly bond.

By the time 2014 had rolled around, Yusuf was again living in Dallas as a result of having gotten married in 2008. When I told him that I'd be moving to Dallas for my job, he was surprised but excited. As a kind and generous man who loves helping people, he pledged to help me in any way possible once I arrived. True to form, he helped me purchase everything I needed for my new apartment. And, maybe more importantly, he made sure I ate at all the best Mexican-food restaurants.

Whenever I hung out with Yusuf and his wife, I have to admit to feeling jealous. I wanted what they had, but I knew that my wife—who wasn't even my wife yet—was thousands of miles and hundreds of pages of legal-work away from me. I was beyond grateful for my new position as Senior ICB Pricing Manager supporting AT&T's wholesale segment. But now that I'd overcome that obstacle—with the help of many friends and colleagues—I was ready for my next great challenge.

Ever since my return to the states, Shankaron and I spoke on the phone every week, if not more often. I remember one fateful day when traffic was bumper-to-bumper while I was on my way to work in Raleigh. Because no one was going anywhere, I decided to call my sweetheart. But, as I was dialing her international number, which takes a few more seconds than dialing a domestic call, I slammed into the SUV in front of me. It had started to go but had abruptly stopped. Because I was focused on my call and not on my driving, I hadn't noticed it stopping until it was too late. Thankfully, no one was hurt in the accident.

When I finally had the opportunity to call Shankaron later that day, I told her, "I got into an accident because of you."

She didn't think it was funny.

After seven months of long-distance phone calls, Shankaron agreed to take our relationship to the ultimate stage. She was ready to get married.

Much later, I would learn that two handsome profile photos of myself that I'd sent her may have been what tipped her from friend to love interest. She said, "When I saw your photos, I was done. I knew you were for me." She printed those photos and kept them with her during our prolonged and unwanted separation. And, while I had instantly liked her upon our first meeting, she'd sent me photos of herself as well, which made me fall in love with her even more. I couldn't wait for us to be husband and wife, but distance and legalities would prevent that from happening for far too long.

After Shankaron agreed to marry me, she introduced her mother to me—on the phone. I told her mother that I loved her daughter and very much wanted to marry her. Thankfully, her mother gave me her blessing, but with the addendum, "so long as that's what Shankaron wants."

Gratefully, Shankaron immediately chimed in. "Yes, mother. This is what I want. I love Abdi, too."

Our engagement ceremony, known as a *nikah*, took place in Mogadishu on August 21, 2014, with Shankaron, her family, and my family all in attendance—and with me still living in Irving, Texas. It would have been difficult for me to have flown back to Mogadishu at that time, so they celebrated our engagement without me.

Stranger things had happened to me than that.

My plan following our engagement party was to meet Shankaron in Mombasa, Kenya, marry her, and then spend our honeymoon there.

But, of course, such a trip would have its difficulties. They always did.

———

Because any flight to Mombasa from the US would require a layover, I landed at London's Heathrow Airport on August 30, 2014. Because I had multiple family members living in London, I chose for my layover to be three days long.

In fact, my dear sister Dhuuh was still living there. Like so many of the family members I'd seen in Mogadishu on my last trip there, I hadn't seen Dhuuh in twenty years. When last I'd seen her in Kenya, she was young, energetic, and gorgeous. I wondered what she'd look like after two decades and six kids. Then I wondered if she'd even recognize me after so long—though the wheelchair was probably a giveaway.

As soon as I exited the plane and my phone connected to the nearest Wi-Fi network, my sister called. "Hello, my dear brother! Have you arrived yet?"

"I just got off the plane. Just getting through the customs check."

"We've been here for two hours! Get out here now! We can't wait any longer!"

"I'll be out soon. Promise! I can't wait either. But don't rush me and make me fall out of my chair!"

She laughed, and in that laugh I heard the world's most welcoming sound.

About thirty minutes later (What can you expect at customs?), I arrived at the waiting area. Before I could even look around and get my bearings, my sister and her daughter, Maryama, were rushing to me. They bent down and hugged me, then kissed me on the cheek.

I said, "Oh, sister, you look almost the same. You haven't changed much." I grinned. "Look at me, though. I have changed a lot. My hair has started to turn gray and I'm losing hair on the front of my head!" The last time she'd seen me, I was a skinny, hurting, yet surprisingly resilient sixteen-year-old.

Her reply surprised me, but she was always a generous soul. "You look fit, actually!"

From then on, we carried on as if we hadn't missed a step in our relationship, even though we'd missed thousands. She introduced me to her husband, Omar, whom I'd never met in person but had spoken to a few times over the years. He fetched their car, then we were off to their home in Enfield, just north of London.

Once we arrived, I was overwhelmed with gladness and love. My younger sister, Yasmin, was there. She'd been ten when last I'd seen her—

just a girl. Now she was thirty-one, a beautiful woman raising two beautiful daughters of her own. She lived with her husband in a neighborhood that was ten minutes' drive from Dhuuh's house. Had Yasmin not come to Omar and Dhuuh's house, I don't think I would have recognized her.

The following day, my dearly departed sister Ureeji's widower, Saeed, visited us. He and I had spoken often back when he'd lived in Addis Ababa. When he first saw me in London, his words surprised me too.

"Abdi, you look much younger than you sound on the phone."

I thought, *Maybe my care and compassion make me sound like a wise, old man on the phone. Or maybe I'm just fit these days because I want to look my best for Shankaron.* Either way, I thanked him for the compliment.

I also met Farhan, my younger brother. He'd been five when I'd left Mogadishu! When I saw him, all I could say was, "What a man you turned out to be!" We spoke at length concerning what he was doing with his life: pursuing a bachelor's degree in computing at a college in London. I was thrilled for his success and his future—another example of why my parents had instilled in us a sense of duty to help one another. My sister Dhuuh helped Yasmin and, in turn, Yasmin helped Farhan immigrate to London to create a brighter future for himself.

I will forever cherish that beautiful day reconnecting with my siblings and family. But I had to leave. I apologized for not being able to stay longer. I promised to visit soon and spend more than just a few days. We gave each other tearful goodbyes and hugs and kisses. It was yet another trip that was far too short but had been very fulfilling.

Early on September 4, 2014, I flew from London to Nairobi, Kenya, where I'd stay for one night before heading on to Mombasa.

It was about time I started my own family.

18 Paradise Found

My cousin Mohamed Hashi greeted me upon my 2 a.m. arrival at Jomo Kenyatta International Airport in Nairobi. Knowing that I had to depart for Mombasa at noon the next day, I asked if he could bring his siblings to my hotel room. He gladly obliged, and I had yet another layover where I was able to meet a Warsame family I hadn't seen before. I was glad for the opportunity, but my future bride and my future life awaited me in Mombasa. I couldn't wait to board that plane.

Then, of course, as soon as I got to the terminal where my plane was departing from, an announcement rang out. My flight would be delayed for at least an hour. I was frustrated, to say the least, and I was worried that the flight might experience further delays. I just needed to travel one last leg of this trip, and now this!

During the wait, an older man sat next to me. I scrutinized his face because he looked familiar. Eventually, I realized who was sitting by me: Mohamed Yusuf Haji, the former Minister of Defense in Kenya. A male staffer assisted him, and I'd later notice his security guard. I guess I must have been staring for too long as he turned to me and, in Somali, said, "Hello."

I replied and introduced myself, then I peppered him with questions regarding Somalia's affairs. Since none of us were going anywhere soon, he seemed open to talking, and I wasn't going to waste an opportunity like that to talk to someone who had been deeply involved in the events surrounding my birth country.

In so many words, he essentially said that Somalia's government was weak, but it needed more international support to extend its authority throughout the country. He burnished Kenya's image by stating how his country had "done its part" by hosting the largest number of Somali refugees. He then reminded me that he and his fellow Kenyan officials were always encouraging Somali officials to continue with their reconciliation process.

I asked, "What do you think about Somalia's regional leaders meeting with officials in neighboring countries, in Kenya and Ethiopia? Does that further weaken the authority of Somalia's central government?"

He replied that, given where Somalia had come from (i.e., the civil war) and the resultant disintegration of all aspects of Somali society, it's not unusual to see such friction still in existence. But the Somali government must overcome their past through present dialogue.

I nodded and then kept asking questions. In 2010, Kenya had adopted a new constitution that called for a federal system similar to the system in the United States. I wanted to know his thoughts about such a drastic change. "How is the newly instituted federal system working for Kenya?"

He replied by regaling me with the time he'd visited the United States as the Provincial Commissioner of Garissa. He'd witnessed firsthand how state and local governments were run in relation to the federal government. Just as he was about to tell me whether he liked the system or not, a voice blared through our waiting area.

Our plane to Mombasa was now boarding.

An hour later, I landed.

———

Have I mentioned that I have family in every corner of the world? Well, not *every* corner, but they seem to live in all the places I've ever visited. Mombasa was no different. My cousin Noah picked me up from the airport. Like so many other family members I knew who lived far from me, I'd spoken to Noah on the phone, but I'd never met him in person until that day. Even though we didn't know each other all that well, I knew he would do everything he could to make me feel at home.

I also knew that Noah was likely having a hard time when I landed. His brother, Awais, had been struck by a truck near the Kenya–Uganda border just a week prior to my arrival. He did not survive. Awais had been in his mid-twenties. He wasn't married and had no children. It deeply saddened me to think about such a promising young man being lost too soon. I was grateful to Noah for taking me under his wing in Mombasa, even while he was still dealing with the loss of his dear brother. Being with Noah reminded me what I had long forgotten: don't take today for granted.

After vainly searching for an hour for a wheelchair-accessible hotel, we discovered the Bridge Hotel. Even though my room wasn't particularly appealing, I could get into and out of the bathroom. Plus, I was hungry and exhausted. All I wanted to do by that point was eat and get to bed. Noah went to the hotel's restaurant and brought us back a full dinner of chapatti, chicken, and vegetables, and passion fruit drinks. He and I talked some more before he departed, saying he'd be back in the morning.

That's when a strange feeling came over me, one I hadn't felt in decades. Alone in a foreign country, in a strange place, without a phone, I was fearful. The city of Mombasa felt unsafe to me. I asked myself why I'd come there instead of staying in Nairobi. I was so fearful that I even began doubting my trip to Kenya. Had I rushed my decision?

My limitations, which I so rarely thought about, became glaringly obvious. If someone were to enter my room with bad intentions, what could I really do to them? If I needed medical help of any kind, how would I get it? Every latent fear I'd had as someone who had to rely on his wheelchair came to the forefront of my mind as I struggled to sleep in that foreboding hotel room. Eventually, my mental and physical exhaustion overtook me and I fell asleep.

The next morning, I awoke early, showered, and prayed. Noah arrived soon thereafter and asked how I liked the place. I was honest and flatly replied, "It's OK."

He could tell I wasn't thrilled. "What can we do?"

"Do you think we could look for another place, a nicer place for me to welcome my new wife?"

"Yes, of course. We will look around."

"I'm considering going back to Nairobi."

"Why?" He seemed genuinely shocked. "Don't do that, Abdi. We will find you and your new wife a better place to stay. I'm sorry that this one isn't working out."

He seemed somewhat hurt by my statements, so I explained why I felt uneasy about this hotel. "It's not your fault, cousin. Most hotels' first floors are for multipurpose use. They don't typically have elevators here. They don't think about accessibility for people like me."

He nodded his head. "I understand."

We walked—I rolled—to a nearby restaurant for breakfast. Unfortunately, the entrance to the establishment was covered in dirty water. As if to underscore what I'd just said about the lack of accessibility, the tires on my wheelchair tracked mud into the restaurant. Had a ramp existed, that wouldn't have been a problem.

While dining, Noah thought to call his uncle, who knew Mombasa well. He'd help us find a hotel that was both excellent and wheelchair-accessible.

I didn't bother to tell him that those two descriptors meant the same thing in my book.

His uncle suggested the Paradise Resort Apartments. Even when I just overheard the name of the place, I thought, *That's it. That sounds perfect.*

Noah agreed with his uncle, saying out loud, "Yes, that's a good place. I hadn't thought of it."

As fate would have it, his uncle even knew the owner and would make a call to him on my behalf.

Minutes later, Noah's uncle called us back. "They have a fully furnished one-bedroom unit available for five hundred dollars a month."

I'd planned to be there for two weeks, but I ended up being there for thirty days, so it turned out to be exactly what I needed.

Noah and I left breakfast and immediately drove to Paradise.

As we approached, I saw that the apartment was in an upscale Nyali neighborhood and was near the beach. I saw signs for 24/7 security. The building looked pristine and the landscaping was well-kept. I immediately loved the place.

Noah's uncle awaited us there. He and the apartment's owner greeted us. Unsurprisingly, the owner was a fellow Somali. After speaking with them and thanking them for the help, I rolled into my new room. With an air conditioner, fully equipped kitchen, TV, Wi-Fi, couch, and queen-size bed, the room *was* paradise. It made me forget every regret that had assailed me the night before.

And it's a good thing I found paradise. I'd have to wait ten days before Shankaron arrived from Mogadishu.

19 Honeymoon in Mombasa

During that ten-day, unwanted waiting period, Noah asked, "What's the status on your wife's visa?"

"Nothing seems to be happening. I think it's becoming less and less likely that it will even be issued." I don't think he expected such an honest response.

Prior to leaving Dallas, I'd contacted my cousin Mohamed in Nairobi. He was a travel agent for the Euro-Africa Travel Group and knew what I'd need to do to get a visa for my wife. He told me it wouldn't take longer than a week for her to receive it. I sent him the required fee and hoped that Shankaron would be with me just a few days after my arrival in Kenya.

Noah broke into my thoughts. "What if she never comes? What if your whole trip is a waste of money?"

I replied with silence. I hadn't thought of that possibility. *She may never come! What if the visa doesn't come through? It's already been a week!*

After collecting myself, I had to admit that Noah was right. "Indeed, the trip will have been a waste if I can't get Shankaron to Mombasa. She's the reason I've come so far!"

I had another fitful night of rest. I couldn't shake Noah's questions. If Shankaron never arrived, I'd have to return to Dallas without seeing my wife or enjoying our planned honeymoon. My doubts even said it was possible that our marriage could be over. If we could never live together, and if thousands of miles would always separate us, could we remain married? For the first time in a long time, I considered that my bright hope for tomorrow—of a better future with my stunning wife—might be dimming. I was beginning to lose hope.

The next morning, I called Mohamed for an update. Truth be told, I'd called Mohamed every day for an update during that waiting period. He knew how excited and anxious I was about getting Shankaron's visa. He'd placed a more senior employee on the task, but I'd lost hope in her. Maybe she wasn't prioritizing us, or maybe the case was somehow proving problematic. She gave Mohamed new promises every day, but another day would pass with no progress. When I called Mohamed that day, I told him that I desperately needed to hear a good answer from the senior employee working on our case.

He replied, "Then you will be glad to hear that she secured your wife's visa just this morning."

I was thrilled. "Book her a flight in two days from Mogadishu to Nairobi!" It wasn't a question so much as the release of internal pressure that had been steadily building within me over the last eight days. I wanted to give her a little bit of time, so she spent some time shopping and getting ready to meet a man she'd met in person only once before: me

Although Shankaron didn't have much time to prepare for her visit, she was equally thrilled that the paperwork had gone through. She left Mogadishu on September 13, 2014, and arrived at Jomo Kenyatta in Nairobi a few hours later. Mohamed greeted her, then gave her a ticket for the last leg of her trip, from Nairobi to Mombasa. Her flight would leave at 5 p.m. that day.

At 6 p.m. on September 13, 2014, dozens of travelers from Mombasa filtered through the doors at the Nairobi airport. My anxiety mounted as more and more people walked by me. Had I forgotten what my bride looked like?

As soon as I was almost about to give up hope, I saw Shankaron walking toward me. She looked nervous, and who could blame her? In addition to meeting me for only the second time, I'd later learn that she'd never traveled outside of Mogadishu and its surrounding areas before.

I rushed to her as soon as I saw her. We hugged. After so many months apart and so many, many phone calls, I couldn't believe she was finally with me. The future I'd always envisioned for myself was now standing right next to me. I hoped and prayed that would always be the case.

After departing the airport, we stopped at a mosque to pray, but Shankaron stayed in the car. She was tired after having traveled from Mogadishu to Nairobi to Mombasa. After our drive to Paradise, I asked, "What do you think of Mombasa?"

"My first impression? Honestly? It's not that great."

"Well, you haven't seen much of the city yet, so don't give away your hopes." I smiled as reassuringly as I could. Mombasa had to grow on me as well.

We dined well that night. Shankaron and I didn't stop talking for what felt like hours. The following day, we celebrated our new marriage with friends and family at the Paradise Resort.

One man attended the party whom I didn't know. He came up to me and asked, "Do you recognize me, Abdi?"

"Absolutely not." I couldn't remember the man at all. I wasn't sure if he were joking with me or not.

"Do you remember the family who gave your father that piece of land in Ifo to set up his tent?"

My eyes went wide with understanding. "Yes! Yes, I do. Of course." It had been nineteen years since I'd seen this man who had done a seemingly small thing for us but whose simple generosity had impacted the rest of my life. I thanked him for what he'd done for our family.

Many other friends came to the party and wished us well. Even my younger sister Ilhan was able to attend. She hadn't even been born before I'd left for the US!

Our apartment was full of the sounds of family. I was so grateful for each one of them and thrilled that they'd gotten to meet Shankaron.

Following the celebration, Shankaron and I had one final task ahead of us before we could relax as husband and wife: getting us both back to America.

––––––––––––––

One difficulty with international travel is that it can get expensive very quickly. I was spending three thousand Kenyan shillings a day for a rental car, equivalent to one hundred US dollars every three days. I was also spending another twenty to thirty dollars per day on food. Then there were the added expenses of the room, the flights, the parties, and the shopping.

But, in hindsight, I can't say I cared all that much. After such a long time of taking care of others, it was time to take care of myself and my wife. Every expense was worth it!

While in Mombasa, I ran out of vacation time. I knew it was a possibility, but nothing meant more to me than meeting my wife and enjoying her company for as long as I could. I called my boss and asked if there were any possible way that I could work remotely from Mombasa for the next three weeks. My boss graciously allowed me to do so, and I was even sent less complex cases during my time there. My boss and my colleagues all knew how important this trip was to me, and I remain grateful for their generosity to me during that time.

Almost every evening, Shankaron and I would dine out. We particularly enjoyed the Nairobi Java House with its outdoor setting, fantastic staff, and exceptional food. On one memorable weekend night, we went to the Mombasa Beach Hotel with Noah and his wife. This place was a truly magnificent hotel that overlooked the Indian Ocean—another slice of paradise not far from our Paradise. They would often have live music, and I recall hearing superb African music when we arrived.

But what made this outing memorable wasn't the impressive setting; it was the staff. As we were coming near the hotel, I saw a curve that I couldn't quite figure out how to navigate with my wheelchair. I thought a wheelchair ramp might be just beyond its bend, but when I was close enough, I saw no ramp. This was not a surprising development in Africa. Most places didn't have the accessibility accommodations that are so prevalent in America. I waited there for a moment, trying to figure out how to get to where I needed to go. I could travel the world by myself, but sometimes the smallest of distances provided me with the greatest of problems.

That's when an observant staffer noticed my conundrum. Without saying a word, he darted into the hotel and then brought out a few pieces of what looked like handcrafted wood. He assembled the pieces to create a perfectly made ramp, which he set down before me. I was amazed and gave him my thanks as I immediately rolled up and through that now-accessible curve. I wished more places in Africa were accessible, or at least had more staffers who would take quick notice of our particular needs, but in that moment, I was grateful for that small bit of assistance to help me get further into paradise.

Unfortunately, earthly paradise doesn't last forever. My wife and I departed Mombasa for Nairobi on October 5, 2014. We stayed in Nairobi for the next five days, neither of us wanting to admit that we would have to be apart yet again before we could finally be together, full-time, in the United States. During those five days of bliss, I had arranged for her to stay with—you guessed it—a relative of mine in the city. Shankaron had asked to wait on her US visa while living in Nairobi. Thinking that she might have to wait just a few weeks, and maybe a month or two, I agreed.

After a tearful good-bye, I left Nairobi on Friday, October 10, 2014. After nearly a month-and-a-half of vacation that had overflowed with family, friends, and new love, I was simultaneously tired and rejuvenated by the time I arrived back at my apartment in Irving.

I returned to work the following Monday, but my real work would happen after 5 p.m.

I had to get my wife to the states.

20 The End and The Beginning

Two weeks after returning from Kenya, I mailed Shankaron's visa application package to the U.S. Citizenship and Immigration Services (USCIS). I'd needed that much time to compile everything I had to send in on her behalf: our marriage and birth certificates, a copy of her Somali passport and my US passport, proof that we had lived together in Kenya, an I-130 form, a.k.a., the Petition for Alien Relative, a G-325a form, a.k.a., the Biographic Information (for Deferred Action), and the $420 filing fee.

They received the application package on November 3, 2014. I'd read of others in my same position who had hired lawyers at great expense so as to avoid lengthy delays or possible rejection due to missing information or improper filing. Even with their help, the process could still take over a year. I was cautiously optimistic that I'd included every requested item and Shankaron's visa would be arriving within six months.

Of course, I'm always cautiously optimistic.

While we waited for word from the US government as to whether my wife could finally join me in the states, I continued working hard at my job with AT&T. To prepare for her new life with me in Texas, Shankaron had enrolled in English classes at Atlas College in Nairobi. And we spoke nearly every night on the phone.

Early on in our immigration process, I told Shankaron that I thought she might be able to join me that summer, within the far too optimistic timeframe of six months. But Shankaron is more reserved and practical when it comes to such matters. Though she did not say it outright, I could hear the doubt in her voice. She didn't think her visa would come through so soon.

The USCIS approved her application in March 2015. But that wasn't the end of the process. Once approved, our application was sent to the National Visa Center (NVC) at the U.S. State Department. At that point, I received a notice from the NVC requiring me to pay an affidavit of support fee of $120 and a visa application fee of $325. I couldn't imagine having to pay a lawyer thousands of dollars on top of what just the filing fees were amounting to be. But, keeping my beloved in mind, I gladly accepted these incidental costs.

This part of the process required more paperwork as well: three years of IRS transcripts, my Social Security earnings statement, six months of pay-stubs, proof of employment, and more. I also had to complete yet another application form via the NVC's website. However—of course—the form I needed to complete was unavailable that day due to technical difficulties on the website. I completed it later, but that small difficulty delayed the processing of the visa package by at least a month.

I am a patient man, but I have to admit to becoming impatient with this laborious process. I understood why it was necessary, but I wished the process could somehow be easier. Honestly, after so long apart, I just wanted my wife with me again. I wanted our new lives to start as soon as possible.

On August 6, 2015, I received an early morning email from the NVC: "All documentation necessary to complete the National Visa Center's processing of your case has been received. As soon as an interview date has been scheduled, the petitioner [me] will be notified. The applicant should NOT make any travel arrangements, sell property, or give up employment until the US Embassy or Consulate General has issued a visa." This was indeed great news. I called my wife to let her know that her visa application had finally been approved, nine months after we'd first started the process.

But the process wasn't over. In fact, the hardest part was our next step, and my dear wife would have to take that step by herself. Following a medical examination (another $320), Shankaron would have to be interviewed, one-on-one, by a governmental employee at the U.S. Embassy in Nairobi.

To call these discussions interviews is being nice. Many people referred to them as interrogations. The officials conducting the interviews would ask tough, rapid-fire questions, trying to ascertain an applicant's truthfulness behind their motivation to enter the US. And while the official is worried about possible terrorists lying their way into the country, most of the applicants are filled with anxiety because their stakes could never be higher. One wrong answer and a process that has required months of work, money, and patience could be all for nothing.

Shankaron was no different than any other applicant. She knew that if she failed the interview, her hopes and dreams of reuniting with me would be lost. Consequently, prior to her interview, I peppered her with practice questions. The problem with that is that no one knows exactly what questions might be asked. Still, I hoped that our practice interviews would help her compose herself during the actual interview.

She was initially scheduled for her formal interview on October 27, but it was pushed back by three days. To make matters even more maddening, her interview was set to take place at 6:30 a.m., meaning that she'd have to hail a cab around 5:30 a.m. in order to make it to the Embassy on time. Despite such an inconvenience, Shankaron didn't complain and made it to the Embassy on time. For security reasons, her cell phone was confiscated at the gate, which she thought nothing of—until the interview.

Shankaron would later tell me all about her nightmare experience. As she walked into the waiting area, she saw people exiting their interviews in tears, certain that they'd failed their interviews. Others knew they hadn't passed and had been flatly denied entrance into the US. Shankaron's already heightened anxiety increased, right before she stepped into her own interview.

The interviewer began by asking basic questions: "How did you meet your husband? Where did you meet him?"

Shankaron answered appropriately.

Then the interviewer began to dig deeper. "Has Mr. Warsame been married before? Does he have children?"

Shankaron replied, "No, he has not been married, and no, he does not have children."

"Why hasn't he married someone by now?"

In hindsight, I assume this question was asked because of our age difference, but Shankaron didn't think about that at the time. She replied, "That question confuses me. I don't know why he wasn't married before."

Sensing the first possible "crack" in Shankaron's testimony, the interviewer then tried to verify my wife's words. The officer scanned Shankaron's documents and then asked, "Do you have any evidence proving that your relationship with Mr. Warsame is factual? Any text or call history?"

Nervously, Shankaron replied, "They confiscated my phone at the gate. And I didn't know to print out our call records."

"Mmmhmm. OK."

Shankaron knew something was wrong. She sat in silence.

"Do you have a Kenyan police certificate of good conduct?"

"No. I didn't know I would need that, but I've never been in trouble."

"You still need it."

"I understand."

The interviewer ruffled a few papers and looked at my wife. "That concludes our interview. You will need to submit the missing information we discussed—text and call records with your husband and a certificate of good conduct—before receiving our decision." The interviewer handed her a piece of paper.

Shankaron glanced at the paper and felt her heart drop. She exited the interview without saying another word, then texted me immediately afterward: "I didn't pass."

I replied, "What happened?"

She texted a photo of the paper the interviewer had given her, which said her visa had been denied. However, the paper also said she was denied due to missing information. In other words, she'd been denied only for that part of the interview, and not for the entire process. We just had to get more paperwork in order.

But Shankaron didn't see it that way, and I couldn't blame her. The elongated immigration process had taken its toll on her as well, and the intensive interview was the last straw. She told me that she'd lost faith in the process. She feared that her immigrating to the United States was never going to happen. It was just too hard. When she thought she'd been fully denied, she recollected stories of other would-be US immigrants she knew who'd been denied and whose appeals had dragged on for years.

We were finally able to speak to one another later that day.

With a sadness in her voice that I could immediately hear, she said, "I've lost all hope, Abdi. I can't go through that process again. It was terrible."

"It will work out fine, dear. I promise you. I know it's hard, but the struggle is worth it. I promise." To be honest, at that moment, hearing my wife so downtrodden, I wasn't sure I fully believed what I was saying. I was losing hope as well. Obstacle after obstacle had been placed before us on this immigrant journey. There was no guarantee that she'd receive a visa. And if that didn't happen, our chances of ever living together would be impossible.

Though I loved her, I couldn't entertain the thought of moving back to Africa to be with her. My job was in Dallas, and there was no prospect of an in-company transfer to Kenya. I couldn't just leave my job because my aging, now-ailing parents depended on that income as well. Even if I'd wanted another job, such prospects in Kenya weren't comparable to those in the US. And there was no place I'd rather be than in the United States for obvious reasons: wheelchair accessibility and a much better healthcare infrastructure.

I thought, *Have we met our biggest obstacle? Are we going to lose this race on its absolutely final leg?* Then the thought I never wanted to consider invaded my mind: *Is this the sudden end of our short but beautiful marriage?*

My fears were exacerbated when Shankaron told me she was considering moving back to Mogadishu. Her mother had become ill, and Shankaron was rightly concerned for her health.

But I wasn't ready to let her go. I told her to keep faith with me and that I'd do everything I could to get us through this final, arduous part of our story. In fact, I was so certain that she was going to pass her follow-up interview on October 30 that I asked for two weeks of vacation beginning November 16. I knew I'd need those two weeks to show my new wife around her new city—in America.

To get most anything government-related accomplished in Kenya, you need to know someone—or you need to know someone who knows someone. To ensure that Shankaron received her official police certificate of good conduct, I called my niece, with whom my wife was living with during her time in Nairobi. My niece found a man with contacts at the police headquarters. Through that chain, Shankaron received the official validation she didn't know she needed: she was, in fact, a person of good conduct.

Next, I compiled hundreds of pages of our texting and call history, which Shankaron then printed out. She sent that ream of paper and her certificate to the Embassy. Then we waited and hoped and prayed that we'd finally done absolutely everything the right way. This was our last chance to be together.

On December 30, 2015, 422 days after we'd begun the immigration process, I received another email: "Shankaron Nur's visa application documents are ready for pickup at the DHL location at the Village Market

Limuru Road in Nairobi." I read the email multiple times to ensure that what I thought it said is what it actually meant. *Was her visa really awaiting her?*

I immediately called Shankaron and told her to get to the DHL pickup location. She hailed a cab that took her there, but, by the time she arrived, they were closing. They were kind enough to confirm that her package was there. However, she'd have to come back the next morning to get it.

Unbelievable.

Then again, in our story, that's totally believable.

She returned early the next morning, equal parts excitement and trepidation likely coursing through her mind as she tore open the package. I imagine that her smile fell when she saw the first document on top of the stack. It read, "This is not a visa." She fanned through the other documents and thought she saw something akin to a visa, but she wasn't sure. So, she sent me photos of the documents.

When I pulled up my phone early that morning, I saw the first document. "This is not a visa." At that moment, all I thought was, *Oh, God. Please!* Then I carefully flipped through the other documents until something that looked like a visa caught my eye. I scrutinized that document. I read over it multiple times, again to ensure that what I was seeing was really what I was seeing.

This document, placed beneath a stack of papers that had begun with the ominous and confusing notice that "This is not a visa" was, in fact, my wife's much-delayed, highly desired visa.

I suddenly realized it was December 31. What better way to celebrate a new year than to have my new wife join me for our new life together. Now my love would be with me, pushing me, standing by me, loving me, always rolling forward with me into a brighter future I could never have imagined for myself as a young boy from Mogadishu.

Afterword

As of the writing and publishing of this book in late 2018, I am still happily married to my dear wife, Shankaron. Ever since she immigrated to the United States, we have lived in Irving, Texas. Shankaron is planning to pursue a nursing degree at North Lake College. This is not a surprising career choice. She has a big heart for helping people, so it's fitting she has chosen to pursue a nursing degree.

My beloved father passed away in December 2017 after battling a motor neuron disease. "Motor neuron diseases are a group of conditions that cause the nerves in the spine and brain to progressively lose function. They are a rare but serious and incurable form of progressive neurodegeneration."[15] He was buried in Nairobi at the age of eighty-seven.

My sister Luul lives in Mogadishu with her son, Bilal, and our mother. Luul effectively manages her depression, and she loves being with her son and our mother. My sister and I are the best of friends now!

Because two of my older sisters have suffered from mental illness, mental health issues are close to my heart. For most people, struggling with mental health is a lonely fight, exacerbated by a shortage of psychiatrists, poor clinical facilities, and long appointment scheduling. To me, the whole of mental health care is inefficiently managed. It's shameful for a country as wealthy and powerful as ours to be unable to provide a modern health care system for mental health patients.

---

15   "What is motor neuron disease?" MedicalNewsToday, lost modified January 10, 2018, https://www.medicalnewstoday.com/articles/164342.php

However, I am proud of our AT&T Ability Employee Resource Group (ERG) Dallas – Fort Worth chapter, which hosts monthly family support groups led by my colleagues, Lisa Friedrichs and Paula Waldron, in partnership with the National Alliance on Mental Illness. According to NAMI, "1 in 5 adults in America experiences a mental illness. 90% of those who died by suicide had an underlying mental illness."[16] With mass shootings in America occurring far too often, mental health has become a national crisis.

In addition to my day job as Senior Strategic Pricing Manager, I became the president of the Ability Dallas–Fort Worth chapter in October 2017. Our chapter advances, advocates, and educates on important issues for people with disabilities at AT&T.

Consequently, I have been tasked to assemble a disability advisory panel for AT&T's Discovery District project, a $100-million project designed to renovate AT&T's headquarters in downtown Dallas. The advisory panel will help the Discovery District's design team create an inclusive space for all to enjoy—including those with disabilities. "The centerpiece plaza at Commerce and Akard streets promises to become one of downtown's most popular public spaces. Additions to the area will include 40,000 square feet of restaurants and retail space, a 2-story food hall with balcony dining, outdoor gathering and performance areas and a water garden. A 6-story-tall video wall facing Commerce will be the largest downtown."[17]

We often hear about diversity and inclusion, which is fantastic, but we hardly hear anything about disability inclusion. As you may know, Americans with disabilities account for nearly 20 percent of our population, the biggest consumer group in our country. However, most corporations don't seem to have effective strategies to reach this massive

16   "Mental Health Facts in America," National Alliance on Mental Illness (NAMI), https://www.nami.org/NAMI/media/NAMI-Media/Infographics/GeneralMHFacts.pdf

17   Steve Brown, "See what AT&T plans for its $100 million downtown Dallas Discovery District," Dallas News, last modified May 20, 2018, https://www.dallasnews.com/business/real-estate/2018/05/20/atts-100-million-discovery-district-will-new-draw-downtown-dallas.

consumer group. For example, one thing that baffles me is that most if not all retailers and restaurants don't have someone who can communicate in sign language.

Gratefully, more companies are getting better at disability inclusion. I am pleased to say that AT&T has been on the list of Disability Equality Index's (DEI) Best Places to Work for Disability Inclusion. This index measures key performance indicators such as organizational culture, leadership, accessibility, employment, community engagement, support services, and supplier diversity. Since the ranking began in 2015, AT&T has consistently scored 100 percent.

Disability is the largest protected class yet the least integrated into the workforce. When it comes to hiring and promoting, individuals with disabilities lag behind their peers. Although we have come a long way, there is still much to do.

On August 21, 2018, AT&T hosted a town hall event at their headquarters, where AT&T executives spoke about the company's commitment to disability inclusion. I was honored to present. Among other things, I talked about the contributions that people with disabilities have made to this country and beyond, from Thomas Edison to Franklin Roosevelt, Albert Einstein to Stevie Wonder, to name a few. I discussed irony a lot in this book, and I was reminded of that when I shared about Alexander Graham Bell, who invented the telephone while attempting to convert speech to visual representation in order to accommodate for his wife's hearing loss. Yet, even with those great contributions, there is still a stigma around disabilities.

More than anything, my story reflects the fact that disability doesn't mean inability. My disability didn't prevent me from pursuing big ambitions, such as a career at a Fortune 500 company or business ventures I once attempted that didn't materialize. The point is, I never stopped dreaming for something better and bigger. Neither should you, whether you are someone with disabilities or not. We often undercut our capabilities to achieve something greater.

Remember, if you don't believe in yourself, no one else will. Advocate for yourself and put your best foot forward. I assure you: there is a world that's willing to accept you and ready to work with you at your pace.

Acknowledgments

There have been many people who have helped me bring my story to the world. First, I want to thank my wonderful wife, Shankaron, for her steady support throughout the process. Thank you!

Special thanks to Blake Atwood for his fabulous developmental editing. I'm grateful for the time and efforts you put into refining the storyline. Thank you, Melinda Martin, for the book cover design, and Michelle Marshall, for the book cover photos. Your support and care for this book have been invaluable.

I'd also like to include my sister, Dhuuh, my nieces, Hafsa, Aaisha, Maryama, Asiya, Rahma, and Asma, and my good friend Charlotte Perrone for their book reviews, editorial suggestions, and, above all, their unwavering support through the entire process.

About the Author

ABDI WARSAME is a survivor of Somalia's civil war. Despite being paralyzed from the waist down when he was twelve years old during a rocket attack in Mogadishu, Abdi overcame grave odds to survive his injuries in a place and time where he should have died within days.

Through his Muslim faith, his loving family, and his unrelenting determination, Abdi leapt hurdle after hurdle to become the successful American citizen he is today. In a life full of every reason to quit, Abdi never gave up on himself, his family, or his God.

Believing that education was his only escape from a much more challenging life, Abdi immigrated to the US with his father. While overcoming the language barrier, he took advantage of every opportunity that came his way and ultimately graduated from N.C. State with a B.S. in Supply Chain Management. He has over ten years of expertise in the telecommunications sector. He is a passionate advocate for disability inclusion in the workplace.

Connect with the author and read more at AbdiWarsame.blog.

34726316R00106

Made in the USA
Middletown, DE
29 January 2019